THE HUMAN RIGHT TO A GREEN FUTURE: ENVIRONMENTAL RIGHTS AND INTERGENERATIONAL JUSTICE

This book presents an argument for environmental human rights as the basis of intergenerational environmental justice. It argues that the rights to clean air, water, and soil should be seen as the environmental human rights of both present and future generations. It presents several new conceptualizations central to the development of theories of both human rights and justice, including emergent human rights, reflexive reciprocity as the foundation of justice, and a communitarian foundation for human rights that both protects the rights of future generations and makes possible an international consensus on human rights – beginning with environmental human rights. In the process of making the case for environmental human rights, the book surveys and contributes to the entire field of human rights theory and environmental justice.

Richard P. Hiskes is Professor of Political Science and Senior Political Theorist at the University of Connecticut. He is the Editor of the *Journal of Human Rights* and Associate Director of the Human Rights Institute. He is the author or co-author of four other books, most recently of *Democracy, Risk, and Community: Technological Hazards and the Evolution of Liberalism* (1998). Professor Hiskes has published works on a variety of topics within political theory, human rights theory, environmental ethics, and science and technology policy. He has published articles in many journals, including *Review of Politics, Human Rights Quarterly, Public Affairs Quarterly, Human Rights Review, Hume Studies, Women and Politics, Policy Studies*, and others.

The Human Right to a Green Future

ENVIRONMENTAL RIGHTS AND
INTERGENERATIONAL JUSTICE

RICHARD P. HISKES

University of Connecticut

CAMBRIDGE
UNIVERSITY PRESS

CAMBRIDGE UNIVERSITY PRESS
Cambridge, New York, Melbourne, Madrid, Cape Town, Singapore, São Paulo, Delhi

Cambridge University Press
32 Avenue of the Americas, New York, NY 10013-2473, USA

www.cambridge.org
Information on this title: www.cambridge.org/9780521696142

First published 2009

Printed in the United States of America

A catalog record for this publication is available from the British Library

Library of Congress Cataloging in Publication data

Hiskes, Richard P., 1951–
The human right to a green future : environmental rights and intergenerational justice /
Richard P. Hiskes.
    p.   cm.
Includes bibliographical references and index.
ISBN 978-0-521-87395-6 (hardback) – ISBN 978-0-521-69614-2 (pbk.)
1. Environmental law.   2. Human rights.   I. Title.
K3585.H57   2008
344.04'6–dc22   2008027687

ISBN   978-0-521-87395-6 hardback
ISBN   978-0-521-69614-2 paperback

For Anne D., Anne, and Ben,
in gratitude for
The Presence of the Past
and Future.

Contents

Acknowledgments

All books are, like this one, emergent products of the author's relationships with many others over the course of many years. It is never really possible to acknowledge all the intellectual debts one owes for what appears on subsequent pages, but here is where one attempts the impossible, always in the hope that important contributors are not excluded.

In a significant sense, this book is the product of the Human Rights Program at the University of Connecticut. Although little more than a decade old, the vibrancy, intellectual insight, and enthusiasm encountered daily in interchanges with students, faculty, and staff of the program have richly stimulated the research behind this book and many other current projects at the University. Director Richard A. Wilson, therefore, deserves special gratitude for all that he has accomplished in his short tenure. Thanks also to members of the University administration whose foresight, imagination, and support made the program a reality.

Also deserving of special mention are Professors Alanson Minkler and Shareen Hertel, originators and hosts of the campus-wide intellectual salon, the Economic Rights Group (ERG). I owe a large intellectual debt to all the ERG participants, who discussed, ridiculed, respected, and otherwise fruitfully critiqued the arguments that populate the following pages.

The University of Connecticut provided needed support in terms of time and finances, notably in awarding me the Provost's Research Fellowship. The Department of Political Science, and particularly its Head, Professor Howard Reiter, was gracious in encouraging my scholarly and administrative moves into both the field of human rights and into the campus program. Within that program countless students, both graduate and undergraduate, have influenced the development of the ideas represented in this book. I thank them all. I also benefited from comments offered orally and in print from audience members at the University of Connecticut Humanities Institute, before whom I made the first public presentation of this project.

Several pieces of the following arguments were presented at the American Political Science Association annual meeting, and early versions of them appeared in *Human Rights Quarterly*, *Human Rights Review*, and *Public Affairs Quarterly*. I am grateful both to panel audiences and to anonymous reviewers for their contributions.

Finally, in this endeavor as in all others of my adult life, discussions with my fellow human rights scholar, life partner, and intellectual better half, Professor Anne Hiskes, have been the *sine qua non* of any achievement represented here.

Introduction

Writing a book in a northern climate invariably means looking out the window and witnessing the change of seasons. If the book concerns the environment and the current phenomenon of global warming, writing it leads one to wonder how differently seasonal change will manifest itself years from now (or at least optimistically to hope that seasonal change will continue). As this book lengthened, a different type of season swung into full view – the U.S. presidential campaign, often referred to as the "silly season." What gives this particular season its name has more to do with the current political climate than the natural one, of course, although these days the silliness is partly due to the connection between the two.

The 2008 presidential campaign witnessed no end to the usual list of reciprocal candidate accusations and media "gotcha" opportunities; sadly lacking was much discussion of the whole issue of climate change and what human consumption patterns bode for the environmental predicament of future generations. All of the candidates professed concern about the environment and our impact on it, but none really dared make serious proposals that plotted a path toward saving the planet and ensuring environmental justice for future citizens.

The current politics of environmental preservation – and the lack of political courage that typifies it – is not the primary concern of this book; rather, what the future holds for the convergence of the natural and political worlds is my focus in what follows. This book offers a new set of concepts and a new language with which to bring politics and environmental protection together in the service of preserving for future generations a legacy of clean air, water, and soil. Those three elements I take to be central to any program of environmental preservation, and in this book I argue that together they constitute claims that all citizens, both present and future, ought to have honored as a matter of right.

What follows then is a human rights argument for environmental entitlement to clean air, water, and soil. Not only living citizens possess this
environmental right; I shall contend that future citizens do also, and because
they do the second aspect of my argument is for environmental justice across
generations. As a matter of justice, all citizens present and future possess the
environmental human rights to clean air, water, and soil. Future citizens rely
on these environmental rights of present citizens being protected for the possibility that theirs will be also; more interesting perhaps is that we shall see how
the reverse is also true – the environmental rights of the present depend on
the protection of the rights of future citizens. This reciprocity between present
and future makes environmental justice across generations possible.

Both concepts of intergenerational justice and human rights are newcom-
ers to the politics of environmental preservation. As we shall see, many if not
most scholars have denied that either concept is relevant when it comes to
making environmental decisions. Certainly there are other political and moral
arguments aplenty that encourage the recognition of an environmental obligation, but those arguments are usually framed using concepts like sacrifice,
good citizenship, or stewardship, and invoking a vocabulary from ethics full of
righteous-sounding invocations to "care," to recognize a "moral obligation,"
to "be generous," or "to do one's duty." Surely these are all good words and
sentiments, and they are all guaranteed to move environmental policy to the
rear of any political agenda or presidential campaign bus. Environmentalism
needs a new and more muscular political vocabulary grounded in today's central political ideas of human rights and justice. It must present an argument
rooted in these power words of contemporary politics so that it cannot be
ignored in any election or by any government. This book attempts to supply
that argument and that new vocabulary.

A case for environmental justice that enfranchises future generations and
is grounded in human rights is not an obvious argument, nor is it an easy
one to make. In making it I shall first cut a large swath across human rights
theory today and engage many of the most important discussions taking place
among human rights theorists and practitioners. I shall offer some entirely
new conceptualizations such as "emergent human rights" and also revisit and
redefine some ongoing conceptual disputes, particularly those surrounding
the concepts of group rights and identity politics. I shall also explore the
relationship between the idea of community and human rights, and how the
moral particularism that undergirds communitarianism can be brought into
concert with the universalism of human rights. Along the way I shall also
discuss how nationalism, long considered the antagonist to human rights even
though nation states are the addressees of those rights, can play a role in finally

achieving a universal consensus on the applicability of human rights across the globe and in every culture.

Environmental justice itself is a controversial idea for many philosophers as well and particularly so when placed within an intergenerational context. Environmentalism, I shall argue, invokes a special relationship between present and future generations by linking their interests within an intricate web of responsibility and dependence. It therefore would seem, and most philosophers have argued, that whatever else can characterize the relations between present and future, justice cannot. Philosophers since Aristotle have insisted that justice is a relationship always characterized by reciprocity in some sense; therefore where is the reciprocity between our future generations and ourselves? How is such a relationship with those who do not yet exist even possible? I shall present a novel argument that there is in fact such reciprocity present – I name it "reflexive reciprocity" – and within such a convergence of present and future lies the foundation of intergenerational environmental justice.

My argument ends in Chapters 6 and 7 first with a discussion of how to implement environmental justice by employing environmental human rights, and then how to secure those rights themselves. Both constitutionalism and participatory democracy, it turns out, are requirements for environmental human rights and for environmental justice. The necessities of democracy for human rights and of constitutionalism for justice have been commented on before, but bringing the four together opens new possibilities for institution building and for global policy making concerning rights and justice that have so far remained unanticipated. It becomes then the emerging responsibility of the globe's already established democratic nations to take the lead in pursuing environmental justice and human rights, and in the process to continue the spread of constitutional democratic institutions.

Underlying all of the many arguments and conceptual innovations spread across the chapters that follow is one central belief: that politics at all levels is (and should be) increasingly defined in terms of commitments to human rights and justice, and to the spread of both across the globe. As an intellectual or normative commitment this belief can itself be challenged; as a portrayal of the current trajectory of the politics of globalization its accuracy is difficult to dispute. I shall discuss globalization at length in Chapter 5, but what emerges there and from even a cursory examination of any news source of record is that the language of human rights and of justice is the new vocabulary of politics, domestically and internationally. Invoking that language in a new domain of political endeavor that seems daily to be ever more pressingly relevant to our every political interest is not only good philosophy, but good politics as well.

All of politics and life itself is tied to the welfare and general good health of the natural environment that surrounds us. It has always been thus; as a species we are finally realizing it. It is therefore time to let the state of nature back into our political calculations, but our political efforts on behalf of nature need our best arguments. Environmentalism needs the power to persuade that the concepts of human rights and justice have always offered. At the same time, exploring the place of those concepts within the argument for environmental preservation also helps us to uncover new meanings within those concepts themselves. What follows therefore is also an exercise in exploring the conceptual boundaries of human rights and of justice. Those boundaries will be stretched in these chapters, but not, I think, too far.

1

Environmental Human Rights and Intergenerational Justice

I can't help feeling that we are the most wretched ancestors that any future generation could have.

Yehudi Menuhin[1]

The phenomena of global warming and climate change give rise to a singular question: what do the living owe those who come after them? For many thinkers this is a nonsensical query; for others it is simply unanswerable, yet politically it tantalizes in its persistence, especially among environmentalists. As we shall see, the entire cause of environmentalism presumes a connection with and a concern for the claims of future persons that ensure this question a defining place in environmental politics.

As a question invoking the language of justice, many philosophers follow the eighteenth-century philosopher David Hume in his disdain for even asking it, and liberal theorists of justice have been on the defensive ever since. Hume ridiculed social contractarians for believing that the circumstances of justice could be met in a relationship between a living generation and one that either no longer existed or did not yet exist. His logic, at first glance anyway, seems impeccable: it has always been difficult to envision real obligations owed to persons whose nonexistence makes their claims irrelevant in both law and logic. Nevertheless, the twenty-first-century concerns surrounding environmental degradation have revived the need for a convincing argument to protect future generations. This book seeks that argument within the muscular language of human rights, specifically the human rights that together constitute "environmental human rights."

---

[1] Violinist Yehudi Menuhin in a conversation with Dr. Jonas Salk, broadcast on PBS-TV, 27 September, 1982. Quoted in Terence Ball (1985), "The Incoherence of Intergenerational Justice," **Inquiry**, 28, p. 334.

JUSTICE, HUMAN RIGHTS, AND THE PASSAGE OF TIME

Before we can make the case for an intergenerational sense of environmental justice based on human rights, there are many definitional issues of justice and human rights, and their possible relation, whose answers might explain how environmental human rights can serve as the medium of intergenerational justice. Even exploring briefly what others have said on these issues cuts a large swath across several fields of moral, legal, and political philosophy. First, concerning justice, many scholars agree with Beckerman (1999) and Ball (1985), who simply deny that justice can be construed as relevant within a cross-generational context. Both follow Hume's logic that because justice is a matter of reciprocal obligations, it can only pertain to living beings.

Furthermore, when focusing on the concept of justice, we should be careful not to confuse what Sheldon Wolin (1960, 2004) might call "the presence of the past" with the more tangible debt owed to the future. As a historian of political theory, Wolin is referring mostly to what honor or respect we owe to past generations for their legacy of ideas and knowledge. Brian Barry (1999) recognizes that the question of environmental justice across generations raises the possibility that we shall owe much more – and of a more tangible nature – than mere reverence to future generations. He therefore admonishes that at the very least we should recognize that intergenerational justice is a potentially misleading term, because scholars use it "as a sort of short hand for 'justice between the present generation and future generations.'" He is correct that time's arrow does render it impossible to alter the relative justice of our relations with past generations, but others would insist, following Hume, that a similar impossibility persists governing relations of justice between present and future.

The second broad area of definitional controversy involves our understanding of human rights. The employment of human rights as the mechanism of intergenerational justice is similarly fraught with conceptual and logical hurdles. Even if we sidestep all of the inflated rhetoric of the abortion debate, speaking of the rights of future generations seems to do violence to the whole concept of rights as the property of living persons. Especially because rights are typically viewed as the property of individual persons (although, as we shall see, this is controversial as well), it is intrinsically difficult to picture real persons many generations down the road whose rights should restrict our behavior today. Even if we construe the justice relation in general as primarily a matter of rights – another controversial move – we would still have to explain why the rights of potential persons (or groups) should function as claims against the living within our considerations of justice today.

Other scholars have begun to make the argument that I attempt to realize more fully in this book. Recent work by James Nickel (1993), Joseph Sax (1990), and Edith Brown Weiss (1989) has argued that environmental concerns offer a role for human rights within intergenerational justice. Nickel presents a case for what he calls cross-generational "rights to a safe environment." Sax recognizes how different such rights are (and would have to be) from traditional human rights, and Weiss introduces "planetary rights" as environmental human rights that work to protect the future's interests. These arguments represent initial attempts to bring together the concepts of human rights and justice while recognizing that both must be alternately stretched and compressed to make room for each other, given their different emphases on individual persons or groups, negative liberty or equality, and the living versus the not yet born.

It is not difficult to see why some authors have attempted to bring the language of human rights into their case for environmental protection, sustainability, and justice. As a category of speech, "human rights" has increasingly become the lingua franca of politics in many areas, and with considerable success in other battles over justice, such as those involving racism or the oppression of women, or in the transition from genocide to political equality. Since the acceptance of the Universal Declaration of Human Rights (UDHR) in 1948, the concepts of human rights have increasingly been accepted as norms governing the behavior of states. As Risse, Ropp, and Sikkink (1999, 4) argue, "human rights norms are well institutionalized in international regimes and organizations." Therefore the usefulness of employing the language and, for Risse et al., the "power of human rights" in the pursuit of environmental causes should not be very surprising.

This particular convergence of human rights and justice theory in an argument to preserve the environmental welfare of future generations is difficult to sustain (both for these authors and in this book) for a variety of reasons having to do with the nature both of rights and of justice and because of how they have traditionally been construed by philosophers and political thinkers. This means that the argument that unfolds in the following chapters will engage us in reinterpreting, and in some cases seriously challenging, many traditional beliefs or positions within moral and political philosophy. The results of these challenges are several conceptual innovations in how we should understand both the nature of rights and the demands or circumstances of justice. I anticipate here only a few of the arguments engaged more fully in later chapters.

First are the arguments against the idea of universal moral rights in general, including traditional utilitarian arguments such as Bentham's that insist that all rights are creatures of law and therefore are limited in scope to contexts in which they are enforceable by recognizable agents such as governments. Thus, the idea of a universal moral right where enforcement is not defined and the persons with corresponding duties are not prescribed is, famously for Bentham, "nonsense upon stilts." The utilitarian critique of universal moral rights (whether "natural rights" in the eighteenth century or "human rights" today) is still relevant today, especially within current debates over universalism versus cultural relativism regarding whether rights really are universal or merely "Western."

More recently, some rights theorists have claimed that because rights (and/or the duties that they imply) always conflict and are therefore not "compossible" or compatible with each other in a legal sense, any notion of rights must be more local and contingent than is generally considered acceptable by advocates of rights as foundational principles. For instance, Dowding and van Hees (2003, 292) conclude, "[T]he noncompossibility of rights is an embarrassment especially to those who want to argue that rights form the foundation or basis of justice." Because I am specifically exploring the role of human rights in justice across generations, rights' noncompossibility seems a powerful obstacle.

A second area of difficulty in presenting an argument for intergenerational justice based on environmental human rights lies in the still "second-class" status of environmental rights compared with more "fundamental" human rights. Many theorists and commentators, if they acknowledge environmental human rights at all, would relegate them to the conceptual category known as "social and economic rights." These are generally considered to be secondary rights, if they are considered rights at all. Sometimes arguing for such rights, which include many from the latter half of the UDHR, is referred to as promoting "positive" rights. We shall discuss the alleged difference between negative and positive rights in Chapter 2; suffice it to say here that positive rights are said to be less "fundamental" because they require more from governments or others than merely noninterference, that is, actual aid, such as educational facilities, health care, or welfare transfer payments. Such rights seem less basic than, say, the right to life or to be free from torture, because governments and peoples still disagree on the degree to which they should be met or to which they threaten other "more basic" rights, such as to liberty or property. Environmental human rights on the surface seem similar to such economic and social rights that appear as somehow secondary – on our rights wish list perhaps, but probably not even near the top.

Shari Collins-Chobanian (2000, 135) argues persuasively that on the other hand, even the most fundamental "right to life" presumes prior and therefore more basic "rights to clean air, water, and soil." Still, the impression persists that Maurice Cranston's famous (1967) division of human rights into "real and supposed" categories downgrades environmental rights to the level of the other social and economic rights that make up the latter thirteen articles of the UDHR.

The argument for environmental human rights that emerges in the following chapters also insists that environmental rights are ineluctably group rights, attached to future persons viewed abstractly as members of particular, although abstract, groups. In this I am following Weiss, but with the recognition that construing environmental human rights as the rights of future generations makes them therefore subject to all the arguments against viewing such group rights as "real" human rights. Group human rights, as we shall see in Chapter 3, are a topic of much contemporary controversy within human rights scholarship today. The fact that logically it is impossible to view the environmental rights of future generations as anything other than group rights makes my task even more daunting.

Finally, the concept of justice across generations presents its own panoply of problems. Hume's critique of social contract theory is worth recalling here, but more recently the variety and sheer multiplicity of criticisms of Rawls's (1971) argument that justice requires a "just saving principle" are also relevant. Environmentalism has its army of advocates to be sure, and its current rallying cry of "sustainability" might indeed be, as Richard Norgaard claims, "primarily an issue of intergenerational equity."[2] Nevertheless, if Terence Ball (1985) is correct that the whole idea of intergenerational justice is intrinsically incoherent, my basing it on what many consider to be the tenuous foundation of environmental (group) human rights would not seem to make it any more coherent or persuasive. Ball's assertion follows that of others in claiming that because justice intrinsically requires some type of reciprocity between individual persons, the whole idea of having reciprocal relations with persons who do not yet exist is clearly spurious. As Peter Laslett and James S. Fishkin (1992, 7) summarize, "individuals are in reciprocal relationship with their contemporaries, but with their contemporaries only." I argue in Chapter 3 that basing intergenerational justice on the environmental rights of future generations brings a unique kind of reciprocity between present and future citizens that, although unusual, is correctly viewed as real reciprocity nevertheless.

Therefore, there are plenty of preliminary reasons to suspect the conceptual cohesiveness and power of the argument that follows. Part of my response is to suggest and explore some conceptual innovations about rights and justice, exploring the possibility that our understanding of both must grow to

---

[2] Quoted in Beckerman (1997).

embrace "emergent" features implicit but up to now mostly ignored by modern approaches to rights and justice. If the argument succeeds, however, there is potentially a large payoff of benefit, especially to advocates of human rights. If environmental rights of future generations can be maintained and intergenerational justice can be based on them, I contend in Chapter 5 that we have hit on a set of human rights that can be adhered to by all societies, regardless of their relative cultural differences. Although those differences persist within a globalizing world, all cultures presume the existence of successor generations of their own national or "blood community." I therefore contend in Chapter 4 that there are built-in reasons for respecting the environmental rights of clean air, water, and soil for at least the future citizens of one's *own* country, no matter which rights other societies protect for their future citizens. Whether this might be a welcome solution to the consensus/diversity debate within human rights theory – or just another opportunity for jingoistic national self-concern – is a matter I take up in the discussion of how to implement environmental rights and justice in Chapter 6.

The rest of this chapter considers three issues foundational to the arguments presented in later chapters. They all concern what can properly be contained in a theory of justice rather than, for instance, in a larger theory of morals but outside the bounds specifically of justice. The first issue asks whether justice is applicable to future (or past) generations in any real sense, or alternatively, although obligations to other generations might be required morally in terms of respect or of supererogation, if they do not fall under the demands of justice. The second issue challenges whether environmental goods are properly contained in a theory of distributive justice at all, since they appear, at least superficially, to be quite different from the usual objects of distribution within any theory of justice. They are collective – I use the term *emergent* – goods rather than individually assignable ones; as such they are usually not contained in liberal justice theories. Finally, the third issue asks the questions why should justice be specifically about the distribution of rights, and, even if it is, why should justice extend specifically to environmental rights?

JUSTICE AND THE FUTURE

Although some theorists of justice, such as Weiss (1989), include the notion of justice toward past generations, most accept Barry's judgment that the concept of intergenerational justice realistically concerns only the duties of present generations to those of the future. I follow Barry's injunction as well and speak primarily of what justice requires in terms of our obligations to the future. Traditionally since Aristotle and running forward through Locke and most liberal justice theorists, philosophers have viewed any moral obligations to future persons or generations as "supererogatory"; that is, they arise because of a general duty to be altruistic or humane rather than from the actual requirements of justice.

The main difference between supererogatory duties and those required by justice is that the former are not enforceable on free people without taking away their autonomy in choosing whether to be moral. Because most moral theories agree with Immanuel Kant's eighteenth-century insistence that individual persons are capable of morality *because* they are by nature autonomous, duties that attenuate autonomy cannot be morally required. They might still be moral in nature – in fact they might indicate a heightened moral sense or a "better" person – but only if they are freely chosen.

Justice differs from altruism or supererogation precisely because it can and should be collectively enforced on individual persons, even though in modern philosophy the coercion is assumed to be self-imposed by democratic choice. Enforceability in morality, however, presumes that certain conditions characterize the preexisting relations between people who are covered by the rules of justice. Those conditions were first elaborated by Hume and have been accepted by most prominent liberal justice theorists, including Rawls, Dworkin, Gauthier, and Barry. Rawls (1971) names the conditions identified by Hume as the "circumstances of justice" and argues that unless they are present, justice is not possible.

Hume and Rawls argue that it only makes sense to characterize a relationship as eligible for the application of justice principles if three elements (circumstances) pertain. First, it must be a relationship roughly between equals. Second, the goods that persons seek and concerning which justice principles are needed must be relatively scarce. Third and following from the first two, the relationship is characterized by a conflict of interests between parties who are admittedly self-concerned (or just selfish), because all want the same goods (and are equally capable of acquiring them), but scarcity prevents all from obtaining them in equal measure, much less in the amounts perhaps desired. If these conditions do not pertain, then Hume and Rawls conclude that the circumstance is not one of justice but likely of either war on the one hand or humanistic charity on the other. Neither resides in the moral space occupied by justice.

What Hume and others, especially Rawls (1971) and Barry (1989, 1995, 1999), conclude is that no relationship involving present and future generations can manifest all three conditions or circumstances, and therefore justice cannot be established between them. The particular sticking point is the first, that of rough equality. Whether scarcity and conflict will persist is an empirical question for future generations to explore, and perhaps resolve. What cannot be altered, according to Barry (1989, 189), is the effect of time's arrow:

> Whether or not the circumstances of justice obtain among nations is an empirical matter. They may or they may not. Whether or not they obtain between the generation of those currently alive at one time and their successors is a logical matter. They cannot. The directionality of time guarantees that, while those now alive can make their successors better or worse off, those successors cannot do anything to help or harm the current generation.

I argue in Chapter 3 that in fact successor generations can provide a kind of reciprocally beneficial effect for the living, although strictly speaking Barry is right, in the sense that what I call "reflexive reciprocity" requires the current generation actively to articulate what the benefit coming from the future will be.

For the moment, however, we should recognize that although both Rawls and Barry support policies that purport to protect the interests of future generations, on examination neither can presume that such policies are required as a matter of justice. Barry (1989, 202) points out that Rawls's "just saving principle" depends not on principles of justice but on "motivational assumptions" regarding the "actual sentiments of natural concern that people have for their successors." These assumptions show that Rawls's case for preserving resources for future generations is grounded in emotions such as care and simple humanity or altruism, not in justice. In Barry's case, while ultimately rejecting that justice depends on Hume's "circumstances," he (1999, 104) nevertheless supports sustainability policies on behalf of future generations not on the grounds of justice but on "some notion of equal opportunity across generations." Even he admits that conclusion represents little more than a call for further study into the "notoriously treacherous" concept of equality, rather than of justice. For both thinkers, then, protecting the environment for those who succeed us is a matter not enforceable as a duty defined by justice; rather, it is a laudatory charitable act they would like to persuade us to perform.

Kristin Shrader-Frechette (2002) responds to Barry's call and adapts what she terms the *Principle of Prima Facie Political Equality* (PPFPE) as the axiomatic basis of environmental justice between generations. Shrader-Frechette makes clear that "environmental justice" refers to both a specialized meaning of justice and a movement. Both manifest "the attempt to equalize the burdens of pollution, noxious development, and resource depletion" (p. 6). Thus, environmental justice does postulate a form of equality between generations, and as such it seeks "a connection between environmental exploitation and human exploitation" (Tartar in Adamson, Evans and Stein, 2002, 214). For

Shrader-Frechette, the first condition of justice therefore is met even in a cross-generational context, but only in the special case of environmental justice.

We shall return to Shrader-Frechette's concept of environmental justice in the next section, but what is important here is her attempt to adapt an idea of equality to cover the relations between generations. Doing so allows her to make an argument for a duty to future generations on the grounds of an axiom of equality contained within her specialized conception of "environmental" justice, even if it does not extend to a more general concept of social justice.

However, attempts like Shrader-Frechette's raise the general issue of why it should it matter so much whether obligations to future generations are grounded in requirements of justice rather than in our commitments to other principles such as equality (Barry, Shrader-Frechette) or in our emotional commitments to those who come after us. Why is the "extended humanitarianism" principle of Wilfred Beckerman (1999) or John Passmore's "chain of love" stretching to our own posterity not sufficient to protect future generations? The answer is that such normative commitments and emotional sentiments, however laudable, cannot claim the universal applicability and enforceability that Hume recognized as separating justice from what he termed *sympathy*. Sympathy, like Beckerman's normative commitments, Passmore's intergenerational love, and Rawls's motivational assumptions about one's concern for successors, is too particularistic or narrow in its focus to function as a general principle for savings required by justice.

For Hume, sympathy dissipated as one became further removed from its particular objects, as in the case of walking away from someone in distress or viewing the suffering of someone to whom one is only distantly related. Only justice, with its analytical and juridical universality and power, is not susceptible to the motivational, ethical, or sentimental vagaries of individual persons or to the distances (in either time or space) between them. Equality (stipulated as an axiom), love, and humanitarianism might indeed move many to care about the welfare of future generations; only justice can claim that *all* must do so, and not out of a shared sense of altruism or humanity but because of shared moral and legal principles governing ownership and distribution of resources.

So, if a principle of justice to protect the welfare of those who come after us is required but apparently not forthcoming, given the difficulties of achieving qualifying intergenerational circumstances of justice on the one hand and the weakness of relying on our particularistic attitudes (both normative and affective) on the other, what prospect is there for the emergence of such a principle? What we need is a principle of justice that rises above its time-bound circumstances to embrace the future without doing so by relying solely on normative commitments to equality defended merely as an axiom (Barry, 1999, 99; Shrader-Frechette, 2002) or on emotional sentiments (Passmore, Rawls).

COMMUNITIES OF (AND FOR) JUSTICE

Avner de-Shalit (1995) makes a start on supplying such a principle of justice by introducing the concept of the "transgenerational community."[3] This notion of a community that "extends into the future" (p. 12) contains a powerful obligation to future generations as members also of our present community, to whom we owe consideration of their interests as a matter of right. This community is, in Sandel's (1982) and Taylor's (1989) sense, truly "constitutive" of self-identity but with a new twist. For Sandel and Taylor (and, for that matter, Edmund Burke), their conservative sense of community was constitutive of identity through its connection to past generations; for de-Shalit, it is our communal connection with future generations that constitutes our identity today, both as citizens and as individual persons. In recognizing our justice obligations to future generations, therefore, we are serving ourselves.

> I am claiming here that the constitutive community extends over several generations and into the future, and that just as many people think of the past as part of what constitutes their 'selves,' they do and should regard the *future* as part of their 'selves.' These are the relations that form the transgenerational community, which is the source of our obligations to future generations. (1995, 15–16; emphasis de-Shalit's)

For de-Shalit as for Sandel, the possibility of a truly constitutive community relies on more than merely shared sentiments; it must include, as for Sandel, "the shared self-understandings of the participants and embodied in their institutional arrangements."[4] This shared self-understanding or sense of communal identity is manifested in three ways: through daily interpersonal interaction, through cultural interaction, and most important, through the recognition of what de-Shalit calls (p. 22) "moral similarity." Although daily interaction and cultural interaction cannot include future generations of a

---

[3] De-Shalit is not the first to explore the idea of community as including future generations. For an interesting discussion of the obligations to future members of one's own "moral community" that can be expected to share the same conception of the good, see Martin P. Golding, "Obligations to Future Generations," *The Monist*, 56 (January 1972), reprinted in Ernest Partridge, ed., (1981), *Responsibilities to Future Generations*, Prometheus. De-Shalit's approach focuses more clearly on communal identity than does Golding's, an approach shared by Holmes Rolston III in "The River of Life: Past, Present, and Future," in Partridge.

[4] De-Shalit (1995, 33). De-Shalit is quoting Sandel (1982, 173).

community, for de-Shalit moral similarity clearly can and does. This is important because daily and cultural interaction only deliver an "instinctive" sense of belonging to the community, whereas the recognition of moral similarity requires rational reflection and choice (p. 43). The recognition of future generations as participating members of the community then is based not only on humanitarian or emotional impulses but also on rational self-interest.

It is through self-interested reflection that contemporary community members include future members in consideration of current decisions, and, presuming their moral similarity to themselves, adopt principles of justice to guide current decisions that include the welfare of future members as well. For de-Shalit these decisions are justice decisions, so that justice assumes an intergenerational element as a necessary part of the shared moral similarity that defines the community as a whole.

De-Shalit's argument is a novel and compelling one that helps to form a basis for the argument presented in Chapter 4, that environmental justice communities cognizant of their duties to future generations should use nationalism and shared political citizenship as their organizing principles. It also lays important groundwork for a conception of justice that delivers an obligation to future generations for reasons more demanding than supererogation, general humanitarianism, or affective attachments. Thus it represents real progress in justice theory's ability to establish the grounds for a concept of intergenerational justice that clearly includes, as we shall see in the next section, the preservation of environmental goods.

Given its communitarian basis, however, de-Shalit's approach must also include a notion of the communal "good" that defines the community and *only* that community. De-Shalit acknowledges (p. 124ff) as much, agreeing with Sandel and Taylor in recognizing the necessary role of such a shared conception of the good of the community. In so doing he opens his approach up to an important criticism lodged by Barry, one of particular relevance to the argument that I make in Chapter 4 of this book.

Barry (1999, 99) expresses the concern that because of its communitarian basis, transgenerational justice delivers rationality-based obligations to future generations of one's own particular community *only* by ignoring the welfare of other future communities, to which one's successors will not belong. This is a problem, Barry claims, because de-Shalit's theory "cannot offer any reason for people in rich countries to cut back so as to improve the prospects of future people in other communities." De-Shalit's communitarian approach, in Barry's words, succeeds only too well in closing the gap between the welfare concerns of a particular community's present and future citizens. The problem, Barry claims, is that "the most important thing for a theory of intergenerational justice to deliver" is left out: the obligations that the present community has not only to its own future citizens, but to *all* future communities.

Barry's critique is important and to be expected from an advocate of a universalist theory of justice when confronted with a communitarian one, yet it overlooks an important aspect of all communities, one that de-Shalit does not emphasize and that I do not fully explore until Chapter 4. It is true that any communitarian theory such as de-Shalit's argues only for the justice obligations of each community for its own successor generations. If we presume that part of every national or cultural community, no matter how different in other ways, is a shared sense of its own successor generations, then a theory of intergenerational justice such as de-Shalit's has a universal impact. True, it is an appeal that works only for a community in consideration of its obligations of justice to its own future generations, but it makes the appeal to *every* community to act in such a way.

Our conclusion then, one explored fully in Chapter 5, is that although all communities might not (and probably will not) make the *same* provision for future generations, they all will make some and will do so on the grounds of justice. As we shall see in Chapter 4, that is an important step to take in terms of intergenerational justice, particularly so for those concerned with environmental justice across generations. It is to the difficulties of including environmental issues within a concept of justice that we must now turn.

ENVIRONMENTAL GOODS (AND "BADS") AS THE CONCERNS OF JUSTICE

So far, my argument for environmental human rights has turned on an argument for building a strong sense of community in societies within which the rights of present and future generations of citizens to a safe environment can be protected and furthered. This places somewhat novel demands on the concept of community within both liberal and conservative understandings of the term but also suggests a rather paradoxical consequence. It is at least ironic to rely on communitarianism to build an argument specifically for *environmental* justice, because the actions of single communities would seem at least initially to be the wrong focus for environmental issues. Clean air, water, and soil are not particularly benefits that a community on its own can guarantee either to its own successor generations or even its current citizens. Pollution is no respecter of political or even geographic borders, especially when it comes to air and water. Furthermore, what continues as the most discussed environmental issue today – global warming – carries in its name an implicit rebuke to those who view environmental issues in too communal – that is, too local – a fashion. Global issues would seem to require global, rather than communal, responses.

What environmentalists[5] call "global systemic problems," of which global warming and climate change are but two prominent examples, on first glance do seem to require a more internationalist than communitarian approach for their solutions. Although debate continues about how real these systemic problems are, it is beyond dispute that at least locally – and in many locations – their effects are readily apparent. So how can a communitarian form of justice cope with nonlocal issues like these that connote widespread, systemic environmental degradation today, much less in the future? If the issues are not communal in scope now, why should we presume that a communitarian approach to them will be at all useful to later generations?

Some of the answers to these questions wait upon the discussions in Chapters 4 and 5 of this book. Chapter 4 addresses issues of how communal reciprocity between present and future groups of citizens can lead to global environmentalism, and Chapter 5 argues for how such communalism can build a global consensus on environmental human rights. Before we can even make those cases, however, it is first necessary to explore the preliminary issue of how environmental goods can even be conceived as the distributional objects of justice.

As a final preliminary to addressing the conceptual content of theories of justice to see if they can include environmental products, we should be careful not to dismiss out of hand the "think globally, act locally" appeal of communitarian approaches to environmental issues. As Leslie Pickering Francis (2003) makes clear, it is true that some of the most pressing environmental problems manifest both local and global causes; still, the existence of the latter does not render the former irrelevant. Furthermore, steps taken on the global level to remedy the situation do not invalidate local efforts, nor do they relieve communities of their own moral obligation to make such efforts.

Francis uses the example of the degradation of the Everglades ecosystem in Florida. The threatened condition of this unique subenvironment is thought to be caused both by local encroachment through economic development as well as by the effects of global warming, chiefly rising water levels in the oceans that threaten to transform, even submerge, the Everglades. The administration of George W. Bush supported restoration efforts aimed at combating the local effects of encroachment by developed lands, but at the same time refused to

---

5 See Leslie Pickering Francis (2003), "Global Systemic Problems and Interconnected Duties," **Environmental Ethics** 25, 115–128. Francis gives credit to Robin Attfield (1999), **The Ethics of the Global Environment**, Purdue University Press for the term "global systemic problems" (1999).

sign on to global efforts to combat the phenomenon of global warming, the very existence of which the administration has disputed. The dispiriting question for supporters of both the Everglades and the Kyoto Protocols against global warming (which the Bush Administration refused to sign) then is this: if the global effects of warming continue to threaten overwhelming the Everglades, what is the point of local efforts to restore the area by reclaiming developed lands?

Francis's answer is important for its recognition that both local and global causes and obligations must be acknowledged. The global nature of the problem does not exonerate the local community from its obligation to pursue restoration as a matter of environmental justice. Conversely, those involved in global responses to the local efforts have a reciprocal responsibility at least not to undercut those efforts, and on fairness grounds to help to underwrite them. For reasons of both reciprocity and fairness, Francis (pp. 127–8) claims, justice requires that both communitarian (local) and global ethical obligations be accepted and recognized as interconnected moral duties.

> So a reciprocity argument runs as follows: because we expect you to confer a benefit on us by acting to save the Everglades, we owe you at least that we don't undermine what you are doing in return. A fairness argument would run instead along these lines: you are incurring a cost by restoring the Everglades; it is wrong for us to expect you to incur that cost unless we are obligated to shoulder costs of our own, costs that must be borne if the benefit is to be produced . . . it is important to know that such different moral arguments support interconnected duties.

Francis delivers then at least a preliminary defense of a communitarian approach to justice applied to environmental goods by suggesting that even global environmental issues have important local aspects (both causes *and* obligations) as well. Furthermore, the elements of reciprocity and fairness that she identifies within environmental problems and their potential solutions announce that we are in the realm of justice in exploring how to respond politically. For some, however, this latter supposition is the more controversial – why are environmental goods (or harms) even a matter of concern for justice? Before we explore further the possibility of intergenerational justice, we must defend the proposition that environmental goods are properly the concern of justice, however defined.

David Miller (1999) points out a second paradox about using the communitarian argument for intergenerational justice as it relates to the environment; indeed, for him it is a paradox of any argument involving environmental goods and the future. All such arguments are, he posits (p. 153), "back to front":

that is, any argument to protect the future's claims to environmental goods needs first to "endow members of the present generation with such claims." To accomplish that

> [W]e ought first to show that people in general (whichever generations they belong to) have claims of justice to environmental goods, and then having established the general principle we would move on to consider justice between generations in respect to such goods. But to do this we would need to integrate environmental values into the theory of social justice as it applies to contemporaries.

As Miller notes, most theories of social justice do not take the time to consider either the front or back of the intergenerational environmental justice argument, because they consider environmental issues as occupying a "separate region 'beyond justice'" (p. 151). Similarly, while finding a possible place to address environmental issues within Rawls's theory, Derek Bell (2004, 306) nevertheless agrees with Miller that "Rawls and most other mainstream liberals have completely ignored them."

There are two reasons why most justice theories have not made a place within their general conceptual system for environmental concerns but have instead relegated them to the "movement" (not the theory) called *environmental justice*. John Dryzek (1997, 177) refers to both when characterizing the movement as "concerned with the degree to which the environmental risks generated by industrial society fall most heavily on the poor and ethnic minorities." The first reason is that traditionally, social justice theories focus on goods distributable to individuals, whereas Miller (in Dobson, 1999, 154) admits that this seems not to be the case for environmental goods: "Nobody gets a particular share of the ozone layer or the Siberian tiger." Environmental goods, in short, are collective goods, not always easily distributable as individual shares.

Environmental goods to be distributed are also not always "goods." This is the second reason they are usually omitted from theories of social or distributive justice. Dryzek refers to them as "risks," and Shrader-Frechette (1980, 1993, 2002) makes it very clear that risks are costs, not benefits. The risks presented by pollution, global warming, acid rain, and radioactive wastes are clearly negative effects of living together in the twenty-first century; they are environmental "bads." Because they are often collective rather than individually distributable goods, and because they are equally "bads" as well as goods, environmental outcomes or goals have almost never been included in the theories of social justice from Aristotle to Rawls.

As to the first issue of the collective nature of environmental "goods," Miller is correct in recognizing the clearly traditional, individual impacts of policies that seek to address environmental problems. This would seem to make it important therefore to take justice considerations into account when generating such policies. Furthermore, these impacts carry distributional aspects across individual persons that clearly place them within the purview of justice issues. Although it is true that pollution of the water, air, and soil is an emergent phenomenon, policies generated to address this will have real distributional effects for people, involving their individual liberty, taxation, economic choices, and so forth. Additionally, we should not expect, Miller (p. 154) elaborates, "the impact of these measures to be neutral across persons, for two reasons: the cost will fall more heavily on some people than on others, and the environmental good will benefit some more than others." In other words, these impacts raise traditional issues of distributive justice and should be recognized therefore as important elements of any theory of justice.[6]

The fact that environmental impacts as the objects of justice are often not goods or benefits but rather "bads" or risks of harm also does not alter the fact that they should be seen as essential elements of any theory of justice. Following Rawls, most liberal theories of justice persist in focusing primarily on what Rawls called "primary goods" as the currency of justice in need of a principle of fair distribution. Recently, several thinkers, including Ulrich Beck (1992) and myself (1998), have argued that a more accurate assessment of the contemporary "stuff" of justice would include a prolonged focus on the distribution of risks as harms.

I have argued that it is crucial to understand modern risks as ineluctably collective or emergent in nature, by which I mean that untangling the individual agents, causes, or policies responsible is pointless, if not impossible. That being the case, it is easy to see why the distribution of risks should be approached from a communal perspective specifically focused on justice. Accepting risk as a communal product of a society's collective choices, such as, energy usage and provision, allows us to recognize its distributional effects more clearly. Doing so makes it apparent that managing distribution of risk constitutes a rather large part of a society's commitment to justice.

Environmental risks are, as we shall see in the next chapter, the progenitor of rights precisely because they qualify as the type of harms against which people should have rights. Recognizing the reality of modern risks as emergent,

---

[6] Shrader-Frechette is correct to point out that environmental issues raise not only distributional aspects of justice but also what she terms *participative* elements as well; that is, environmental decisions need – on grounds of justice – to be opened up to participation by all citizens. Along with other thinkers (Hiskes [1998], Dryzek, [1997], and Young [1990]), Shrader-Frechette [2002] seeks to connect the distributive and democratic elements of justice into one singular approach.

collective phenomena – and particularly those represented by environmental hazards – only intensifies the need for individual rights to protect citizens from them. Any theory of justice therefore must be careful to include environmental risks as a major element of distribution and participation. Not to do so threatens to make the whole project of a theory of justice irrelevant in an age characterized by pressing environmental concerns that confront all communities around the globe.

We can therefore conclude that environmental goods (and harms) are intrinsically part of any system of distribution and participation outlined by a theory of justice. Although this appears to be a somewhat novel conclusion given where justice theory has occupied itself since at least Rawls, it is not really a surprising one. *Environmental justice* is a term that has claimed considerable ink both among scholars and journalists in the past decade precisely because of emergent issues like global warming and climate change.

A final area of concern in this chapter then is whether we should explore remedies for environmental harms (and their just distribution) using the language of human rights. Not all justice theorists are comfortable couching arguments for just distributions in terms of individual rights, and this discomfort appears at least initially to be warranted when it comes to environmental rights as responses to risk. Moreover, even if justice is a matter of rights, how those rights relate to the interactions of individual persons with their natural environment and with their successor generations' inherited environment remains as a complexity worthy of our investigation.

HUMAN RIGHTS AND THE COMMUNITY OF JUSTICE

Isaiah Berlin is rightly famous for admonishing that when we seek to understand the interaction of concepts, we should be careful to recognize that "everything is what it is" and nothing else – liberty is not the same thing as equality; morality is not patriotism; justice is not coterminous with rights. Sometimes we have to choose between related but nevertheless discrete values; in those moments it is crucial for both clarity and intellectual honesty that we not attempt to reduce or redefine one of them into another. "The necessity of choosing between absolute claims" is, Berlin concludes (1969, 169), "an inescapable characteristic of the human condition." So far in this chapter I have sought to bring together the concepts of justice, community, and environmental goods; with Berlin's warning still in mind, we must bring one more together with these – the concept of rights. When thinking about obligations to preserve the environment for future generations, is it possible to speak of justice in communal terms and still rely on the claims of human rights?

Chapter 2 is completely given over to a discussion of a new concept of rights that I call "emergent rights," which function as the medium of our environmental obligation to future generations. In the rest of this chapter, to introduce that discussion I shall explore briefly the historically tense relationship among the three concepts of community, justice, and rights.

In the history of philosophy and political theory, the discussion of justice did not begin with the idea of rights, of course, but with community. Both Plato and Aristotle, although differently, framed the question of justice in communal terms, involving individual obligations and benefits to participation in the just community. Besides being construed as a concept applicable only within political communities, justice resided in the theoretical realm of the "good" more than in that of the "right." Hume changed things by exploring justice as a concept governing the rightness of any society's distribution of goods rather than its embrace of *the* good. Justice became less a matter of virtuous participation in the realm of the good than of fair participation in the marketplace.

Although closer to Aristotle's approach than to Plato's, Hume's recasting of justice as a distributional concept both challenged its intimate relationship with community and especially accommodated the new concept of natural right as a measure of one's entitlement to a distributional portion. Hume's theory of justice is still disputed today, but what is indisputable is that in including individual rights as a measure of justice, Hume brought the classical concept of justice into the modern age of politics, a politics dominated by the new language of rights. Because of Hume's revision, subsequent theorists like Rawls would adopt rights as an integral part of the meaning of justice, while downplaying justice's connection to feelings of and participation in the community.

Today there is little debate about the role of rights within theories of justice but considerably more about whether an emphasis on community is consistent with a concern about either justice or rights. Especially in the latter case, critics from Bentham and Marx to contemporary theorists within feminism, communitarianism, neo-conservatism, and postmodernism have argued that the concept of individual moral rights is inconsistent with the goal of community.[7] This raises a particularly thorny concern here, of course: how can a communitarian theory of justice that seeks to accommodate the interests of

---

[7] For instance, see Taylor (1989); Hiskes (1998); Nancy Rosenblum, ed. (1982), **Liberalism and the Moral Life** (Cambridge, MA: Harvard); Michael J. Sandel (1982), **Liberalism and the Limits of Justice** (Cambridge: Cambridge); Jean Bethke Elshtain (1995), **Democracy On Trial** (New York: Basic); Benhabib (1992), **Situating the Self** (New York: Routledge); Judith J. Thomson (1990), **The Realm of Rights** (Cambridge, MA: Harvard); Mary Ann Glendon (1993), **Rights Talk** (New York: Free Press).

future generations as well as present ones be founded on an idea of human rights?

The answer to this question engages all the subsequent chapters and so cannot be answered fully here. By way of introducing what follows, however, it is instructive to focus on the work of Alan Gewirth in contemplating what he calls (1996), somewhat paradoxically it seems, the "community of rights."

For Gewirth, such a community of rights has seemed like an oxymoron to thinkers as divergent as Marx and Bentham to MacIntyre and Glendon, because a focus on rights implies a view of individual persons as "atomic entities existing independent of social ties" (i.e., as "isolated monads" to Marx). Conversely, a focus on community regards individual persons as more or less defined by their "affective social relations with one another" (p. 1). Gewirth proposes to bridge this divide by relying on a concept of human rights that recognizes the intrinsically communal background conditions necessary for any right to exist. Gewirth focuses specifically on two distinct human rights, to freedom and to a certain level of well-being, broadly conceived. These two rights are indisputable, his argument in *Reason and Morality* (1978) concludes and begins anew in *The Community of Rights* (p. 16), owing to the fact that "persons must have and claim these rights because their objects are needed for the very possibility of action and generally successful action."

Accepting these two rights as indisputable carries two general consequences. First, several specific human rights can be seen as constitutive of these two general ones. Gewirth explores five in his book (1996): to productive agency, private property, employment, economic democracy, and political democracy. Second, and of more relevance to my argument, Gewirth claims that these human rights can exist conterminously only with a strong, even constitutive sense of community.

For Gewirth, any society demonstrating a commitment to human rights must accept (or have accepted) certain principles enabling the regime of human rights to succeed. The primary of these is what he terms (1996, 19) the principle of generic consistency (PGC), stating "act in accord with the generic rights of your recipients as well as yourself." The PGC is a logical requirement for all believers in human rights because these claim rights are stipulated for *all* human beings. Thus, "every human has rights to freedom and well-being against all other humans, but every other human also has these rights against him, so that he has correlative duties toward them" (1996, 6). Gewirth characterizes this relationship as one of "mutuality," to be somewhat distinguished from reciprocity (*how* distinguished we shall explore in Chapter 3), and it is this mutuality that makes possible the "conciliation" between the concepts and practices of individual human rights and community.

The universality of human rights, in Gewirth's view, establishes a relationship between persons in a society committed to human rights that is more embracing than that established by mere citizenship rights. This relationship is properly viewed as a genuine community of rights, he claims, for three reasons. First, it requires society to provide for "equal and mutual assistance to secure persons human rights," which it accomplishes by "protecting and promoting the freedom and well-being of all its members" (1996, 82). Second, by accepting such protection, the members "have, recognize, and accept obligations to the society" (p. 83). These obligations are accepted willingly, given what is at stake in receiving the protection (the possibility of freedom and well-being), and lead citizens to acknowledge what is required of them from the second major principle of the community of rights: the *social contribution thesis* (p. 83). Third, citizens' acceptance of the obligations entailed by this thesis is a recognition of how important to their freedom and welfare society's protective function really is. Because society is essentially making possible their agency as free persons, members "develop psychological attitudes of gratitude and loyalty to it, so that it becomes a community of cooperativeness and fellow feeling" (p. 85).

Gewirth's argument is perhaps a bit too sunny in its ability to bring rights and community together, but at the very least it calls attention to how much any appeal to human rights relies on its reception by a group of people who share more common moral and political beliefs than not. In other words, human rights do indeed require a high degree of the "fellow feeling" that most commentators recognize as central to the nature of community. Gewirth goes further (perhaps too far) in establishing the "constitutiveness" of the community of rights, but nevertheless his argument at least opens the possibility that rights and community can share the same political program.

CONCLUSION

We shall return to Gewirth's argument later, but its importance here lies in its establishing the possibility that a society that pursues human rights can indeed be one that is highly communal in nature. If we are to arrive at a concept of human rights that protects – as a matter of justice – the environmental human rights of future generations, we cannot escape the conclusion that only a strongly communal society can do so. As de-Shalit's argument makes clear, only a highly communal society can envision its future generations as participants in its realm of justice. Therefore, if such a society can exist, it will be precisely what Gewirth envisions – a community of human rights.

In the following chapters we shall explore several aspects of this community, including its moral, political, and epistemological commitments. Such a community must appreciate how human rights can change or "emerge" as new threats emerge that threaten the welfare of individual people in a way that properly triggers a rights-based response. It also must appreciate the broadening nature of reciprocity as a requirement for protecting the rights of the future, even admitting the possibility of reciprocity with those not yet born. The community of environmental human rights also must be able to recognize the identity of its future fellow citizens as a group of "people like us," who with us share both moral and political commitments and institutions in common, and therefore who (as a group) deserve the same environmental rights as we do. Finally, the community of environmental human rights must be able to see beyond its borders, because the environmental justice that it seeks to establish as its legacy cannot be achieved alone in a global environment. Thus, environmental justice based on human rights must strive to be the foundation of a global consensus on human rights that embraces all cultures. These are the topics of the chapters that follow.

2

Emergent Human Rights, Identity, Harms, and Duties

I am not disembodied reason. Nor am I Robinson Crusoe, alone upon his island.

Sir Isaiah Berlin, "Two Concepts of Liberty"

With the ratification of the Universal Declaration of Human Rights (UDHR) in 1948, the concept of moral right took on a new modifier: "human." Since the seventeenth century, moral rights had been designated as "natural" (or inalienable) rights and explicitly distinguished from legal or contractual rights. Natural rights did not rely on governments to enforce the law or contracts, according to Locke, Paine, Jefferson, and others; in fact, natural rights in their view predated governments altogether and could be found even in places without government, the so-called state of nature. Natural rights were taken to be universal in the same way that human rights are conceived of today, as we shall see in a moment, but nevertheless the shift in terminology indicates a changing understanding about rights in general. Mostly, the change from "natural" to "human" rights indicates that our view of rights is open to development and growth. I shall rely on this openness to make the case for environmental human rights, which, I argue in this chapter, should be viewed also as "emergent human rights."

The conceptual difference between what we now name "human" rights and the earlier "natural" rights can be overstated, but nevertheless it does call attention to an important development in rights theory. As Waldron (1987) comments, the replacement of "natural" with "human" indicates that moral rights are no longer thoroughly grounded for their justification in certain real or alleged facts about human "nature." In fact, using the term *human rights*, Waldron claims (1987, 163), "leaves open the question of justification, or worse still, takes the mere existence of a broad consensus on these matters to be a sufficient reason for avoiding the task of justification altogether." Not all natural rights theorists bothered with justification either, it should be noted (Tom Paine is a prominent example), and Waldron is probably overstating the rejection of justification.[1] Waldron is correct, however, in suggesting that use of the term *human rights* at least posited a different relationship between the existence of a right and its basis in some feature of human nature. This chapter begins with an exploration of that new relationship, because the acceptability of the idea of emergent human rights in part depends on recognizing the true connection between rights and human nature.

We should begin by viewing several points of agreement between most rights theorists. First, whether regarded as human or natural, today moral rights (in whichever number any particular author is willing to defend) are taken as universal for all humans (Donnelly, 1989; Benhabib, 2002). Their universality stems from their source, which is for the most part logically implied by their necessary role in providing for human dignity (Feinberg, 1980 a, b) and moral agency (Gewirth, 1980). In this aspect, human rights today share the same source as they did in the arguments for natural rights made by seventeenth- and eighteenth-century rights theorists. Human dignity, in other words, is both producer and product of moral rights, in the sense that morality is impossible without them. Because morality (or moral agency) is the unique province of human beings (and which grants them dignity), rights are logically required as "inalienable" for moral systems to be possible (Meyers, 1985).

In addition to their source, most theorists also agree on what the function of rights is; that is, there is wide agreement on what rights "do." They protect – and are necessary for protecting – people from harms (Harman, 1980); therefore, to understand which rights exist, it is worthwhile to ask which harms are threatening enough that humans must be protected from them by means of their rights. We shall ask that specific question in exploring the emergence of environmental rights in this chapter. Moral rights, it is also widely agreed, function as "trumps" in Dworkin's famous (1977) view by providing "the rational basis for a justified demand" (Shue, 1980). For Shue, only certain rights are legitimated as truly human rights on this basis; he terms them "basic rights," a position accepted by most human rights theorists today.

The nomenclature change to "human" rights beginning with the UDHR has added new emphases concerning the operation of rights in the world

---

[1] It is certainly not immediately clear why the change in terminology need necessarily imply a new and totally pragmatic justification for rights, and even if it did, pragmatism does not entirely do away with justification, as Waldron's argument certainly does imply. My argument that follows relies on the changing nature of human relationships from which rights emerge, but it is an open question if those relationships or the change in them are indicative of – or reliant upon – some special feature of human nature.

that are pertinent to our discussion of emergent rights in this chapter. Carl Wellman (in Winston, 1989, 93) limits the number of moral rights by insisting that a human right is specifically "an ethical right of the individual human being vis-à-vis the state." Wellman poses this definition to exclude from the list of actual human rights all other rights held by an individual person against other persons or organizations. This distinction calls attention to the special political history of human rights in the second half of the twentieth century as it has been used as an argument *both* for individual autonomy and national sovereignty. Hannah Arendt (1951, 1979) anticipated this apparent paradox by mid-century:

> From the beginning the paradox involved in the declaration of inalienable human rights was that it reckoned with an "abstract" human being who seemed to exist nowhere. . . . The whole question of human rights, therefore, was quickly and inextricably blended with the question of national emancipation. (quoted in Benhabib, 2002, 151)

Arendt's insight linked the idea of human rights to that of human identity in a new way that I shall explore in the next section, and also anticipated, because of its expressly political character, the recent differentiation between "negative" and "positive" human rights. This distinction invokes as central to the definition of human rights the allegedly differing obligation of government in relation to the two types of rights. Negative human rights are said only to prevent the state from doing something "to" the individual person; positive human rights require the state to do or provide something "for" the person.

The segregation of negative from positive human rights (and the attendant arguments about the correct role of the state) certainly distinguishes human rights from the older concepts of natural rights and also clearly invokes their political character. It is not my intention to resolve the dispute over whether the distinction makes logical or political sense, although I agree with Hobbes that in the real world (not the abstract state of nature), *all* individual rights require government action of some kind for their protection. Stephen Holmes and Cass R. Sunstein (1999, Ch. 1) echo Hobbes's conclusion that in this important sense "all rights are positive." Alan Gewirth (1996, 36) suggests further that the distinction is not as clear as many commentators believe anyway, because many important rights (e.g., to education) are clearly of a third, "mixed" type. For my purposes, a more interesting and basic change than that of positive versus negative rights brought about by a shift in terminology to "human" rights is the unhooking of rights from the seventeenth-century fiction of the state of nature.

To call rights "human" is to recognize their ineluctably social character. This character is important to my argument for seeing some human rights as emergent, because it stresses the relational nature of all rights. Admittedly, some "natural" rights theorists also recognized that at least the practice of rights required the bounds of society, but the possession of "human" rights presumes that we finally leave the myth of the presocial state behind. Anthony Pagden (2003, 192) concurs:

> None of the human rights languages today – indeed no talk of agency and of human personality – would make any sense in some modernized vision of the state of nature, even if we could make such a thing at all persuasive. It is society which observes basic human rights, and it is thus by implication only society which – as the French recognized in 1789 – has the power to confer them.

Although some rights critics persist in attacking rights as "privatizing" (see Glendon, 1991), even the more recent version of the state of nature in Rawls's original position recognizes the relational nature of rights and indeed of all moral concepts. To call rights "human" is to call attention to an aspect of the human personality that uniquely qualifies all human beings to have rights. That feature of human identity that gives rise to rights is one that both produces and is forged in society, amid relationships between people that make moral relations, including those defined by rights, both possible and necessary for the species to thrive. Human identity is defined within human relationships; those relationships produce rights as requirements of moral agency and dignity, without which the relations themselves are not possible.

It is, I shall argue, this relational character of human identity – this unique capacity both to have and to need to have relationships based on mutual dignity and respect for moral agency – that makes the concept of emergent human rights an important aspect of human rights in general. I shall make three arguments in defense of the idea of emergent human rights. First, I shall endorse arguments from feminist, communitarian, and other contemporary approaches to ethics that call attention to this "relational" nature of individual identity. For human rights to be based on such an identity, it must be the case that in a sense and to some probably differing degrees, *all* human rights are emergent in character.

Second, I shall reiterate claims from my previous work (Hiskes, 1998) that a dominant feature of contemporary social and political reality is the existence of "emergent" risks that pose real harm for individual persons. These emergent harms qualify in Shue's sense as productive of rights in that they threaten certain basic human needs. Protection from those harms ought then logically to take the form of "emergent rights."

Third, an essential feature of interaction with the environment, the science of ecology teaches, is the utter "relatedness" or interconnection of factors in the environment and in individual interactions with it. I shall argue that the effects of certain kinds of human interaction with the environment are distinctly "emergent" effects that are usually harmful to both human beings and the natural environment. To the extent that those effects are harmful, they ought to generate human rights for protection from them. It is proper, I shall show, to call these rights "emergent rights," by which I mean specific human rights (to clean air, water, and soil) that have their origin in the group effects of human interaction with the natural environment.

Finally, a particular reason for seeing rights to clean air, water, and soil as emergent rights is based on the traditional relationship between rights and duties as accepted by most philosophers. The duties "correlated" with environmental rights are assignable to individual people not as isolated citizens but only as joint members of a society-wide group; therefore, we shall see why the correlated right must be an emergent one. Furthermore, because of the special connection between present and future generations in their interactions with the environment, those human rights also ought properly to belong to future generations as well.

EMERGENT RIGHTS AND HUMAN IDENTITY

Theories of natural rights began with the state of nature partly to focus the idea of rights within a picture of the human personality untainted by the developmental influences of society. For Hobbes and Locke, human beings possessed rights outside of society because of something in their nature that did not rely on an organized social life to become manifest. Reason was embedded in each individual person as a solitary being, and it is as a solitary being (or "isolated monad" in Marx's famous terminology) that he or she owned certain basic rights. It is this faith in the presence of reason even without the incorporation of the educative effects of social interaction that established a new foundation for natural rights in the seventeenth century and gave to the doctrine its revolutionary character. It is also thus that natural rights theory became associated with liberal individualism of course, an association that continues today.

Human rights, as stated earlier, alter the etymology of rights by calling attention to the social context of rights. Human rights are also more expressly "political" than "natural" rights, because, as Wellman (1995) argues, they presume the existence of governments and stipulate which relations governments should have with their citizens. Therefore, nothing in the UDHR depends on the condition of individual persons outside of – or prior to – states, nor does their possession of human rights depend on citizenship. All persons have rights, and all persons live under governments; neither of these facts implies or denies the other. The possession of human rights does imply something about humans and about human relations that is markedly different than the seventeenth-century basis for natural rights, however.

Human rights as a concept shares with natural rights a foundation in the capacity (and need) of human beings for dignity. The UDHR links dignity immediately with two other features of human identity – our endowment of reason and of conscience. It states:

> All human beings are born free and equal in dignity and rights. They are endowed with reason and conscience and should act towards one another in a spirit of brotherhood. (UDHR, Article 1)

So far this is not much different from the seventeenth-century grounding of rights in the special identity of human beings. As representative of human rights theory generally, however, the UDHR conceptualizes identity differently from the old liberal model by stressing the relations with other people in the development of individual conscience and the protection of individual dignity. Because the idea of human rights does not rely on the state of nature for its notion of identity, it is logical to assume that the identity of individual persons that qualifies them for human rights is one constructed through relations within which the lessons of conscience and dignity are learned.

This new and distinctly *relational* foundation of human identity that gives rise to human rights is an important development in the theory of rights, even though many theorists of identity as well as rights theorists do not make this connection. Not doing so has been a persistent mistake both in several contemporary critiques and in defenses of the idea of human rights.

As a prominent critic of contemporary human rights "foundationalism," Richard Rorty (1993), for example, suggests that the general consequence of relying on human rights to govern moral relationships has been to exclude other cultures who do not share our belief in rationality as the defining mark of our species. Reliance on human rights arguments tends, in Rorty's view, to define the "human" in human nature and rights as "people like us." In Rorty's view, we should better define the special nature of humans as grounded in our heightened ability to "feel for each other" more than do members of other species. Focusing on our moral sentiments – and improving them through what Rorty calls "sentimental education" – would better provide for the goals of security and sympathy than does a reliance on human rights.

Rorty's argument is well known and provocative, but its power as a critique of human rights dissipates if we begin with a conception of human identity not grounded in reason but in the special ability of humans to have relations with each other. Those relations, as we shall see in a moment, are characterized specifically by the kind of "sentiment" and sympathy that Rorty prefers as a basis for morality. If that is so, then it is not the idea of human rights that gets in the way of such moral relationships as Rorty would have us believe. Rather, the problem is an outdated and solipsistic conception of human identity that gives rise to a notion of human rights too much based on the private characteristics of abstractly considered rights holders rather than on what actual persons share together through real human interrelations.

Within human rights theory, Jack Donnelly began the move within political science away from the classical liberal view of identity by insisting that "human nature is a social project as much as it is a given" (1989, 18). Human rights, Donnelly further claims, attach themselves to persons as a social practice aimed at preserving a particular view of human dignity. That dignity is protected through social conventions that grow up around a view of human nature that "emerges out of a wide range of given possibilities through the interaction of natural endowment, individual action, and social institutions" (1989, 18). Donnelly here is reformulating the foundation of human rights on a view of human nature both universal and particular – universal because that nature is grounded on the uniquely human ability to establish moral relations with other persons. Particularity is also part of Donnelly's approach to human nature, in that different cultures with different social institutions potentially will produce a different-looking nature for humans there, given that universal endowment is the same, but social institutions and the individual action that they stimulate will vary.

For Donnelly, this unique interaction between self and others (and institutions) guarantees to all human beings "as human beings" (regardless of cultural difference) protections defined by the changeable nature of their social interactions. It is therefore possible to imagine a universal appreciation of human rights grounded in human identity that still manages to vary across cultures in which human capacities are universally the same, but circumstances differ. This also raises the possibility that human rights are as dynamic as human nature itself, evolving and multiplying in response to "changing ideas of human dignity, the rise of new political forces, technological changes, new techniques of repression, and even past human rights successes" (1989, 26).

Donnelly's reconceptualization of identity to fit what for him is the dynamic nature of human rights is constructed on a crowded platform of twentieth-century ideas about human identity produced by communitarian, neo-pragmatist, and especially feminist theory. Pragmatists like Rorty made it clear that foundational concepts like human nature needed a less abstract and more variegated content to cover the diversity of human experience, especially to encompass nonrationalistic aspects of human behavior such as sentimentality. Donnelly's foundation for human rights, which opens up the concept of human identity to variation depending on social contexts that produce different human relations, fits well with the pragmatist demand for a less abstract view of human nature.

Communitarians also launched a major assault on the rationalistic and abstract view of human nature beginning in the late 1970s, as represented by the work of Michael Sandel and Charles Taylor, among many others. Sandel's (1982) insistence that real community is "constitutive" of individual identity of those it embraces marked a move away from liberal conceptions that viewed community as largely a relationship of shared self-interest, not shared meaning.[2] In *Sources of the Self* (1989), Taylor's acclaimed work on political community and subjectivity, he argues that individual identity is indefinable except in reference to communities of discourse within which the individual lives and derives meaning. He terms such communities "webs of interlocution" and insists that human subjectivity is incoherent as a concept outside them.

> I am a self only in relation to certain interlocutors: in one way in relation to those conversation partners who were essential to my achieving self-definition; in another in relation to those who are not crucial to my continuing grasp of languages of self-understanding – and, of course, these classes may overlap. A self exists only within what I call "webs of interlocution." (p. 36)

Although in many ways opposed to communitarian theory in general, feminist theory owes much to Taylor's emphasis on the relational, collective nature of individual human identity. This debt is evident within feminist theory as it has developed from its early beginnings in moral psychology into its present applications within wide areas of philosophy, political theory, and literary theory. In recent works, both Seyla Benhabib (2002) and Carol C. Gould (2004) trace the feminist views of "intersubjective constitution of the self" (Benhabib, p. 51) and of "embodied politics" (Gould, Ch. 3) to the critique of rationalist liberal identity advanced by communitarian and feminist theorists.

---

[2] See my (1998) discussion of liberal versus communitarian views of the nature of community in **Democracy, Risk and Community: Technological Hazards and the Evolution of Liberalism**, Oxford; Ch. 2.

Of all the contributions of feminist philosophy and political theory in the past 30 years, one of the most significant has to do with how we conceptualize individual identity and/or self-perception. The liberalism of Hobbes, Locke, and Kant insisted on a view of autonomous persons whose self-image was both morally and politically entirely of their own making, a project even capable of being accomplished in isolation in the state of nature. Beginning with the work of Carole Gilligan (1982), Julia Kristeva (1981), Jessica Benjamin (1988), and Sara Ruddick (1989), feminists reconsidered individual moral psychology and development as involving interaction and "connectedness" as a crucial aspect of individual identity and moral development. Gilligan's work elucidated how girls and boys differed significantly in their approach to moral behavior, with girls motivated less by obedience to moral rules and more by relationships and identification with others in need. For Gilligan and Kristeva, this initial difference laid the groundwork for rethinking how gender affects self-image and moral development and also suggested that a new kind of ethics, based on "care" rather than rules, was even more profoundly a new understanding of human personality in relations.

Political theorists and pragmatist philosophers were quick to adapt Gilligan's and Kristeva's insights into a wide-ranging understanding of how a more "relational" picture of individual identity impacts and changes traditional concepts within political theory. The political significance of gender (Benhabib, 1987), the meaning of democracy (Gould, 1988), the problem of evil (Connolly, 1991), the nature of science (Keller, 1983, 1989), the pervasiveness of technological risk (Hiskes, 1998), and even definitions of self-determination within international politics (Young, 2002) were all opened to reinterpretation. Young (2002, 33) summarizes that, contrary to the traditional liberal view of individual persons as "ontologically and morally independent," an accurate description of the meaning of individual liberty and self-determination must take into account that self-identity is "constituted through communicative and interactive relations with others." Furthermore,

> The individual acquires a sense of self from being recognized by others with whom she has relationships; she acts in reference to a complex web of social relations and social effects that both constrain and enable her. On this account, the idea that a person's autonomy exists independent of others and from which they are excluded except through mutual agreements is a dangerous fiction.

This notion of liberty and autonomy develops into a fundamentally different understanding of what makes any particular person unique and therefore worthy of the liberal bestowal of liberty, dignity, and rights. It argues for a view of the self characterized, in Gould's terms, as an "individual-in-relations," or, for pragmatist philosopher M. Johanna Meehan (2001, 232), as "an agent that negotiates its identity intersubjectively within socially specified, shifting parameters." For Gould, what makes each person unique is not his or her internal attributes but his or her unique set of relationships with others. Individual persons remain "ontologically primary" because each person chooses his or her own relations, "but the relations among them are also essential aspects of their being [that] do not exist independently or apart from the individuals who are related. Rather, they are relational properties of these individuals" (p. 148). What I want to suggest is that all human rights are to some extent such "relational properties" of persons, and that some rights – specifically environmental rights – are intrinsically emergent in nature.

All human rights "belong" to each person as a unique individual person, yet they are really "emergent" properties that are visible only in relations with others and in fact are the products of the unique set of individual interrelations that define each person as that unique individual person. As in the seventeenth-century liberal view, rights are intrinsically tied to the uniqueness of human identity, but our view of how that identity is forged has changed. Human beings are unique for their capacity to grow and change through their relations with their environment, both social and physical. Those relationships might be unique for each person and also clearly themselves change through time. Individual people are unique then not as they enter these relationships but as they emerge from the sum of those relationships. It is that emergent uniqueness that makes each person worthy of the dignity and respect that are the objects of human rights, but it is an emergent feature of his or her identity. All human rights then are grounded in the newly recognized "emergent" identity of their individual bearers.

In summary, because of the work of Gilligan, Kristeva, and many others, and embracing the central contributions of Taylor, Habermas, and Foucault, our view of what used to be called *human nature* – and that gave rise to natural rights – has clearly been altered and in turn has altered our view of democracy, science, good and evil, and the nature of risk. We now view all of those features of life as far more "relational" or emergent than we once did. It is time to apply the same understanding to our concept of rights.

Human rights must be seen as emergent first then, because the unique human identity to which they are attached is itself an emergent feature of each rights holder. There are two additional reasons as well: first, because Taylor's "webs of interlocution" are not the only weblike connections between individual people in modern society – their interrelations with their natural environment are also characterized ecologically as emergent; therefore, ecological human rights are the most "basic" of human rights. Second, the harms that threaten individual people in ways traditionally productive of rights to protect those persons are themselves emergent harms. Technological risks are prime examples of these harms, and it is in response to them that we ought to possess human rights. It is to these two arguments that we now turn.

EMERGENT RIGHTS AND ENVIRONMENTAL HARMS

So far we have explored the question of the source of rights and specifically what it now means to say that rights come from human nature, given how our views of human identity and personality have changed since the seventeenth century. Whether they agree on where rights come from, most philosophers agree with Harmon (1980) concerning their purpose: rights function as protections from harms that threaten a person's physical well-being, political equality, or sense of dignity. This is a fairly standard formulation of the operative justification for rights, but to get an accurate picture of which rights individual persons possess, it makes sense also to consider what it is that generates rights as responses to threats, and also what, in their turn, rights produce. In other words, to understand rights in any formulation as responses to harms, we must examine both the nature of the harms that give rise to rights as well as the duties that all rights produce.

Jeremy Bentham and later Joel Feinberg (1980 a, b) referred to this productive aspect of rights as the necessary correspondence or correlation of rights and duties, an idea much criticized today, beginning with H. L. A. Hart's demurral in his seminal "Are There Any Natural Rights?" (1955). In this section, we shall explore the special nature of the harms that generate environmental rights and mark them as emergent rights; the next section explores duties that environmental rights entail on others. We shall see that the duties are also assignable only in an emergent sense.

John Stuart Mill's famous discussion in *On Liberty* (1978 [1869]), concerning the interaction of individual liberty with the potentially harmful effects on others of its exercise, presents a starting point for exploring the second reason to recognize the emergent nature of some human rights – because the harms to which they correspond are themselves emergent phenomena. Mill's argument presents the important libertarian conclusion that "[The] sole end for which mankind are warranted, individually or collectively, in interfering with the liberty of action of any of their number is self-protection. That the only purpose for which power can be rightfully exercised over any member of a civilized community, against his will, is to prevent *harm to others*" (p. 9, emphasis added).

Of course, Mill recognizes (p. 78) that within society any action an individual person takes has real or potential consequences for others, including harmful ones. This is especially true within technologically complex modern societies. Restricting behavior to prevent *all* such conceivable harmful effects is exactly what Mill wishes to avoid in the name of liberty, because society in his view already exercises too much power over the actions and even the thoughts of individual persons. Therefore, Mill contends that the burden of proof must always be on society rather than the individual to prove a case of harm against another person, including a finding that some specific "assignable individual" has been harmed. Anything less constitutes not real harm but merely an "inconvenience... which society can afford to bear, for the sake of the greater good of human freedom" (p. 80).

Mill's harm principle is recognized as important within Western legal and political thought, but his subtler conclusion about what constitutes not harm but mere "inconvenience" is equally significant given the nature of harms within modern technological society. Because Mill's purpose is to defend and extend individual liberty, these inconveniences do not warrant a restriction of individual liberty for Mill, but it is important to see why they do not. It is *not* because they do not impose costs on others; they do – indeed, all individual actions in society have ripple effects that bring costs to others compared with if we all lived in isolation. In the face of inconvenience as the price of a life lived in the presence of others, however, Mill wants us to build a prejudice in favor of protecting liberty. Mill uses as an example the consequences of personal drunkenness – some costs surely accrue to others because of this behavior, but not enough in his view to warrant restriction. Liberty to choose unwisely in personal behavior is an important liberty to protect, even though it has consequences for others. Today we call these consequences of allowable behavior "externalities," and we have a more complicated response to them. I tend to think that if Mill were alive today his response would also be more complex, but nevertheless still fall on the side of liberty. Two more current examples are smoking and, more generally, environmental pollution.

Following Mill and viewed in terms of the risks they impose on others, smoking and pollution would not qualify as harms defined in Feinberg's (1980b, 31–33) sense of "invasions of welfare interests." Such invasions give rise to corresponding rights, but smoking and pollution would not reach the level of harm necessary to generate a right because, taken individually, no single act of smoking or pollution invades someone else's welfare interests in such a way to diminish them "below a tolerable minimum" (p. 33). Therefore Feinberg agrees with Mill that such inconveniences do not justify limiting a smoker's or polluter's liberty by recognizing a corresponding right of someone else not to be subjected to these costs.

Feinberg's Mill-like rejection of a right not to be subjected to smoke or pollution ignores a key feature of those phenomena and the harms that they impose, however. In contrast to Mill's (and Feinberg's) insistently individualistic ontology of the generation of social risks and harms, I have argued elsewhere (1998) that the harms posed by examples like smoking and pollution are better viewed as emergent risks, the harmful products of collective behavior and decisions not usefully reducible to the individual persons, actions, or decisions that generate them. It might be possible to identify *some* of those responsible for smoking or pollution, but realistically these effects are artifacts of countless personal, political, and cultural decisions regarding their acceptability. As such it might be true that no one possesses a right-based claim against any *particular* person for the very real harm of pollution or smoking, but one might still claim a right not to be subjected to such risks or harms. That right would be an emergent right – a protective claim against a harm itself emergent in nature.

Shari Collins-Chobanian (2000) reflects her agreement with this emergent understanding of environmental harms by calling attention to the "cumulative effects" of pollution. Such effects show the narrow outdatedness of Mill's and Feinberg's understanding of the nature of environmental harm, and of the rights necessary to protect people from it.

> Environmental pollution is of a fundamentally different nature than isolatable single-agent threats to our well-being on which he [Feinberg] seems to be relying. While single invasions of our welfare interests – exposure to one toxic substance, some low-level radiation, etc. – *might not* bring us below the minimum level, they all compromise our well-being and might interact to produce cumulative effects. (2000, 136; emphasis Collins-Chobanian's)

Collins-Chobanian's argument in favor of environmental rights is grounded in the emergent nature of environmental impacts that risk harm to individual persons. Although she insists (p. 145) that these are discrete "human, moral rights," not merely a type or subset of a more general right to life, she does not fully appreciate why they are unique rights or why only environmental rights qualify as such uniquely emergent rights, even though in a sense (as concluded earlier in this chapter) all human rights possess emergent elements. Again Mill aids in our understanding of the special and unique emergent status of environmental rights.

In calling attention to the difficulty of protecting individual liberty in society, Mill correctly recognized that the interconnection of citizens within modern technological society produces a persistent tension between free action and the impact of external effects. Had he been a believer in moral rights, this recognition would have convinced Mill of the fundamentally emergent nature of all rights. Instead, as a utilitarian Mill simply (and inevitably) concluded that the idea of moral rights should not be relied on, as he makes clear in *The Subjection of Women*. A less individualistic ontology of identity (e.g., Gould's) would have enabled Mill to maintain both a belief in rights *and* a realization that the intrinsic interconnection of citizens is what makes liberty possible at the same time that it presents unique threats to that liberty. Our identity is a product of our relations with others; therefore, if we are to be free, our liberty must be consistent with that relational nature. This is true in all our relationships and in all aspects of our social life. It is in our relationship with – and effects on – our physical environment that as citizens our interconnection becomes most clear; therefore our rights relating to the environment are uniquely salient for the maintenance of our liberty.

This is a broad claim about the nature and priority of certain human rights and therefore poses the issues of why should environmental rights be both most emergent and most important for liberty? These are separate questions, and the second is most easily answered. Rights to clean air, water, and soil clearly denote essential interests to all people in that, as Collins-Chobanian (2000) notes, they "address the most basic needs of humans; indeed air to breathe, water to drink, and soil to grow food are the prerequisites of all other goals, and are necessary for even taking part in a discussion of goals and rights" (p. 145).

Henry Shue (1980) goes even further than Collins-Chobanian in defending the idea of "basic rights," included in which would be (for Collins-Chobanian and myself) environmental rights. Basic rights guarantee what is "essential to a normal life," Shue claims (p. 29), and in so arguing is reminiscent of Feinberg's discussion of rights as protecting essential interests. Shue also points out, however, that in protecting individual persons against "standard threats," basic rights make the very practice of other rights possible; indeed, the guarantee of basic rights is a prerequisite to the practice of all other rights. In Shue's view, basic rights therefore not only protect the most basic needs or interests of individuals but also provide "a successful defense against a standard threat to rights generally. This is precisely why basic rights are basic. That to which they are rights is needed for the fulfillment of all other rights" (p. 34).

It is hard to imagine any rights more basic either to life or to all other rights than the rights to clean air, water, and soil. Of course, in actual policy decisions, as in daily life, the issue always becomes one of "how clean." This is true of all rights, since the granting of a right never succeeds by itself in resolving such political or pragmatic questions. The right to liberty does not by itself need to answer the question "how much" for us to accept it, as Hart's (1955) argument for a right to liberty as the *only* human right makes clear, and our difficulties in drawing the parameters of the right to free speech leave unchallenged our belief in its necessity.

Even if we acknowledge that rights to clean air, water, and soil are more basic even than the right to life and are therefore more foundational, why treat them as uniquely emergent rights? The answer has to do with who participates in their provision and protection. First of all, environmental rights only "emerge" as rights when social impacts on the environment reach a certain level. When energy sources are threatened with depletion, when degradation of soil, water, and air supplies becomes impossible to ignore, when human knowledge about how life impacts environment and vice versa becomes widespread – with the emergence of these factors in human history comes the understanding of the necessity of environmental rights.

This is not to deny that such rights were always part of the human birthright, nor should we sneer at the seventeenth century's ignorance of them. Our realization of them today required both the complex interdependency and interconnection of life in modern technologic society, and the knowledge that ecology and other modern sciences provide. Environmental rights also waited on what Edith Brown Weiss (1989) calls the "evolution of public conscience" to provide the acknowledgment of moral obligation on which all rights depend. "When this evolution has achieved a certain maturity" sufficient to recognize the practical reality of rights pertaining to the environment, she claims, then "legal obligations and rights are formulated" (p. 103).

In addition, environmental rights are unique for their relationship to time, a point also engaged by Weiss. What she calls "planetary rights" are held by successive generations perceived as groups, who recognize collective obligations to the rights of future generations that can be fulfilled only through collective instrumentalities, that is, governments. In their reliance on government enforcement, planetary rights share a basic feature of all recognized human rights today and also have the same goal: "the welfare and dignity of human beings" (p. 114).

Environmental rights do invoke the future in a unique way, which the next chapter will explore more fully. Even here, however, we can see that Weiss's and Collins-Chobanian's recognition of the "critical mass" of harm necessary for the appearance of environmental rights opens the door to a group or collective aspect for environmental rights. This is part of their emergent aspect in a slightly different sense – as rights that have "emerged" or "come to be" rather than perhaps having always been part of the human experience.

Environmental rights are human rights that have "emerged" in a particular point in human history as the direct result of the growth of human interconnections. They are part of our technological age of global interconnection; they are the product of a shrinking world made closer because of twenty-first-century communications, military, and information technologies. They emerge from our common life and carry duties unlike those of rights from any other period in history. Like all rights, environmental rights invoke duties on others, but who those others are, and how their duties differ from those invoked by earlier rights, are part of the emergent character of environmental rights as well.

ASSIGNABLE DUTIES AND ENVIRONMENTAL RIGHTS

Any discussion of moral rights – especially newly emergent rights – must include careful attention to the relationship of one person's rights to another's duties, if we are to avoid Bentham's castigation of such discussions as "terrorist language." Ultimately, Bentham rejected the notion of moral, imprescriptible rights as dangerous "nonsense on stilts" precisely because of the inability to locate the duties (and their bearers) correlated with so-called natural rights. Failure to identify whose responsibility it is to respond to one's natural rights claims, Bentham insisted, was tantamount to saying it was everyone's duty. Such power of each against all was the prevailing condition in the so-called state of nature, which Bentham preferred to think of as a state of terror.

Philosophers still disagree somewhat on the exact nature of the relationship of moral rights to duties, and Bentham's arguments still loom large. Nevertheless, on two points there is more or less consensus: first, that if there are moral (natural, human) rights, they must imply duties on someone's part to do or refrain from doing something. Second, this relationship is not reversible; that is, all rights imply duties, but not all duties imply rights. There might be duties that people have that are not claimable as rights by some other particular person; that is, they are duties unassigned to any particular right or right holder. For instance, we might all have a duty to give to the poor, but that does not grant any particular poor person the right to demand aid from any particular one of us. These are sometimes called "general" or "supererogatory" duties, to indicate their detachment from any specific right or right holder.

The problem of who acquires assigned duties relating to prescribed rights is particularly pressing within the context of environmental rights, because responsibility for fulfilling duties in response to someone's environmental rights seems diffuse at best, and at worst perhaps only a supererogatory obligation rather than a rights-based one. The emergent character of environmental harms and of the rights to which they give rise is what accentuates the diffuse nature of their correlated duties. Nevertheless, as this section shows, diffuseness of duties does not therefore make us submit to Bentham's insistence that we reject the proposition of environmental human rights.

As stated before, rights exist to protect persons from harms, and therefore they levy duties on others to take action to alleviate the harm or refrain from the harmful action itself. When the harms are diffuse, such as those resulting in violations of environmental rights, the assignability of duties becomes problematic. *Who* has a duty in relationship to someone's environmental right as well as the *distribution* of duty are both complex determinations when the related harm under consideration is the pollution of the air, water, or soil. This is not to deny that large-scale individual polluters can be identified and pursued, but environmental degradation is also a product of countless everyday decisions of all citizens. Some of these are not even conscious decisions, and many of them have histories laden with collective policy choices and social traditions. For example, pollution resulting from the generation of electrical energy can be laid at the feet of local utilities, but surely the blame ought to extend to all of us who use, or rather squander, generated energy. Current energy generation and usage patterns are partly the result of their policy history at state, federal, and local levels. In a democracy, as Shrader-Frechette (2007) has argued, responsibility ultimately lies with all citizens.

All of which raises the issue of how can such amorphous, emergent harms that environmental degradation encompasses give rise to specific rights for specific individual persons? Bentham's warning about granting rights where duties are apparently unassignable keeps coming back to remind us about why rights are so precious: they serve notice that others have duties to protect something essential to our welfare and dignity. If we have difficulty identifying the others who have responsibility to acknowledge our rights and their own concomitant duties, the status of the rights seems jeopardized.

To untangle this problem regarding emergent environmental rights and duties, we should begin with what little clarity there is with which to start. It is clear, as we have seen, that environmental degradation is a harm, and one presenting a basic enough threat to individual welfare to qualify as the basis of a right, as Shue would have it, a "basic" right. Having said that, what we need is a basis on which to determine which responsibility exists on the part of others to acknowledge their duty to aid in protecting me from the risk of environmental degradation. Such acknowledgment of responsibility and acceptance of a duty to protect would function as the correlate of the environmental right, given that we agree that the harm posed is sufficient to qualify for generating rights.

Traditionally among moral philosophers, responsibility of the type we are addressing in relation to harms (that generate rights and therefore duties) invokes the notion of causal efficacy. Following Joel Feinberg, most philosophers agree that if someone is morally responsible (e.g., has a duty) for a harm, it must be true that that person caused it to happen. There is surely a common-sense appeal to this conclusion, especially for those raised in the liberal tradition that what makes people worthy of liberty and rights is their ability to accept responsibility when they cause harm to others. Feinberg (1970, 31ff) elaborates that to assign responsibility it must be possible to determine three things: first, causal contribution; second, that the person responsible was in control of events and that they were not simply random occurrences, the product of some other external causation, or just bad luck; third, that the first two determinations can be "read off the facts or deduced from them; there can be no irreducible element of discretion for the judge" (1970, 33).

When we are discussing environmental harms – and all emergent risks for that matter – Feinberg's criteria for causal efficacy simply cannot be met, at least not completely or without an "irreducible element of discretion." The reason, of course, has to do with their emergent nature. Environmental damage is the result of countless acts of pollution or general abuse, some of which might be traceable to the factory down the road, but much of which is simply the result of millions of people sharing the same space and knowingly or unknowingly having a negative impact on the world around them.

Environmental harms as emergent phenomena are the products both of individual acts and collective ones, some of which are intentional, malicious, or neglectful, the products of conscious decisions either individual or as a polity – and some simply are not any of those things. The cause of such harms might be buried in the distant past, in the long-forgotten decisions of private persons, corporations, or governmental policy–making bodies. In other words, it is not always possible to identify a particular person or persons causally related to the harms, or we simply must admit that we all are to blame. Many environmental harms, in other words, are the product of our life together and cannot be reduced further or their causation assigned any more specifically. Thus, as Marion Smiley (1992) concludes, responsibility over such matters (and distribution of duties as a consequence) is not always as factual a matter as Feinberg claims. Rather, responsibility for such harms, Smiley argues, depends "on a variety of social and political considerations which we either make ourselves or inherit from others in the form of social expectations" (p. 255).

Two conclusions thus far follow from this discussion of environmental harms and moral responsibility. First, we are in the realm of what is known as "collective responsibility" when exploring causal efficacy for environmental damage. Second, our understanding of causal responsibility must be adjusted to fit with the nature of environmental damage; that is, the relationship between causal efficacy and moral responsibility to acknowledge a duty (and therefore establish a right) must be seen as considerably weaker than that demanded by Feinberg. So moral accountability needs a different foundation than that of strict causality – whether I can be said to have caused the harm that creates your environmental rights, I still have duties that correspond to your rights. Furthermore, to arrive at environmental rights as correlates to these duties, the weakened causal efficacy (i.e., diffusely distributed across people and even time) must still be sufficient to generate a right on the part of living persons today to a safe environment.

Collective responsibility as usually construed (French, 1984; May, 1992) identifies collective groups and holds them responsible for which harms can be associated with their behavior. For French, this means that corporations, for instance, should be held responsible for damage that they cause, because as legal entities they can be viewed as actual contractual parties with future generations whose rights are diminished because of corporate decisions. Responsibility can therefore be founded on strict adherence to Feinberg's principle of causality, French argues, because "there are persons that exist now that can have actual relations with the generations of the future. They are corporations or corporation-like entities" (p. 100).

The problem with French's approach is that it is not only corporations that are responsible for environmental degradation, although often we are eager to believe so. As Larry May (1992) points out, some individual members of corporations often deserve to be held more responsible than others, and punishing or holding responsible the entire corporation can often harm individual members who were not complicit. Similarly, Dennis Thompson (1980) refers to what he calls the "problem of many hands," especially within public bureaucracies, to recognize that "many political outcomes are the product of the actions of many different people whose individual contributions may not be identifiable at all, and certainly cannot be distinguished significantly from other people's contributions" (p. 907). It is important for real responsibility, Thompson argues, that even these rather emergent contributions to harm be recognized and their agents held responsible individually and separately from corporate responsibility.

Larry May (1992) refers to arguments such as Thompson's as indicating the presence of a "shared responsibility" that should be seen as distributed to each member of a group engaged in harm-producing behavior. Group membership changes things, May argues, particularly individual members' normal duties and responsibilities. People join groups specifically to enable them to do things they cannot accomplish singly, May points out, and in so doing receive increased ability as a benefit, but "there is also a corresponding cost: members have a special duty to prevent harm caused by their fellow group members, where such preventative acts do not risk significant harm to group members" (1987, 77).

Together, Thompson's and May's accounts of moral responsibility for harms perpetrated by and within groups allows us to envision how such responsibility's relationship to causality is weaker than that insisted on by Feinberg. Within groups, no particular individual might have directly caused a resultant harm but nevertheless could have contributed to it, perhaps in a variety of subtle ways that would be ignored if we held to Feinberg's model. Similarly, as in May's example, participation in groups empowers individual persons to do things – including cause harm – that they could not do alone, therefore responsibility should be "shared" rather than levied solely on the group as a whole.

If May's argument is extended to environmental harms, it is easy to see that for some consequences responsibility should be shared by all members of a society-wide group, because, for example, all have benefited from the provision of electricity by nuclear generation. Does that mean that they all – rather than say the electric company, the public utility board, or the individual members of either – should acknowledge complicit responsibility? Yes. Does the fact that it is difficult to identify all the causal agents of the harm done or the extent of their complicity in the consequences mean that no victim has a rights-based claim to press? No. Weakness of causal efficacy because of its diffusion across an entire society cannot be used to deny responsibility for harms done that violate individual rights. If it could, no rights would be secure in the face of mass behavior such as panic or war.

Environmental rights arise in response to precisely these kinds of harms that are the products of diffuse causal events and a multitude of agents that make any one agent's causal efficacy difficult to prove. So Feinberg's criteria cannot justify them as rights because of the difficulty of assigning duties to particular people, yet they must be seen as qualifying as rights, because the harms that they protect individual people from are truly basic in the way that Shue construed basic rights. This renders environmental rights clearly "emergent" then, because the harms and duties to which they respond are emergent (diffuse across groups and time) as well. Thompson and May help us to see how rights can respond to harms when responsibility is diffuse; in today's globally interconnected world (and environment), it is difficult to imagine which other response rights could possibly represent.

CONCLUSION

The emergent character of moral responsibility for environmental harms completes the picture of why environmental rights are distinctly emergent rights and also why as rights they are unique. We began this chapter with an exploration of human identity that in its current interpretation offers an argument for why *all* rights are emergent. If rights are grounded in (uniquely) human identity, then the character of that identity and its formation are relevant to our understanding of the basis of individual rights. We saw that many interpreters from philosophy, moral psychology, and feminist theory now insist on the relational, emergent nature of human identity; therefore, our understanding of all human rights should include their "relational" or emergent side.

Second, we also saw how the harms that generate rights affect the nature of rights as well. Shue's (and others') insistence that only certain harms rise to the level necessary to generate rights to protect persons from them opens the door to environmental harms and concomitant rights. Environmental harms are clearly emergent in nature; therefore, for this second reason as well we should expect environmental rights to be emergent. Not all rights are in response to such emergent risks, however; therefore, environmental rights are different than other human rights for their expressly emergent genesis.

Finally, if duties are correlated with rights, as most philosophers following Bentham have come to insist, then the quality of the duties associated with rights also affects the nature of the rights themselves. When it comes to environmental harms, responsibility is diffuse across persons, institutions, and time in that they are often the result of years of actions, decisions, or often collective neglect. Strict responsibility for, say, polluted water is always controversial, because its current state is clearly the consequence of "many – and dirty – hands." The harm is real nevertheless and "basic" in Shue's sense; therefore, rights are generated in response to the harm, even though responsibility is collective. Because they are emergent, environmental rights then also invoke duties in a somewhat unconventional way – as collective duty owed by all of society to each individual person to protect his or her rights to clean air, water, and soil.

It is clear, therefore, that environmental rights do exist and are unique for their expressly emergent character, even compared with other rights held by modern people with their "relationally" defined identities. In their emergent nature and their unique relationship to time, environmental rights invoke the possibility of intergenerational justice at least as it pertains to environmental protection and sustainability, but how solid a foundation for intergenerational justice these rights can provide depends on more than the three arguments about their emergent character explored so far. In addition, one more element common to all theories of justice since Hume must be explored – the requirement of reciprocity as a central feature of justice between any set of agents. If reciprocity is necessary to transform an imperfect obligation of environmental stewardship into one founded on rights, in which sense can we speak of reciprocity within environmental obligations to the future? It is to that question that we now turn.

3

Reflexive Reciprocity and Intergenerational Environmental Justice

It is not the office of a man to receive gifts. How dare you give them? We wish to be self-sustained. We do not quite forgive a giver. The hand that feeds us is in some danger of being bitten.

Ralph Waldo Emerson, "Gifts"

As pointed out in Chapter 1, theories of justice, especially contractually based ones such as those presented by Rawls, Gauthier, Barry, or Nozick, do not, in Wilfred Beckerman's (1997) phrase, "time-travel very well" (p. 395). In other words, moral consideration of future generations typically is not an essential feature of such theories owing to the fact that relations with the future cannot meet what Hume called the "circumstances of justice." Although all of these theories (and especially Rawls's) acknowledge obligations to the future, these obligations are held to be outside the demands of justice. In other words, although being concerned for the future might be proof of moral uprightness, justice in particular does not actually require us to care about future generations. Keeping such future-oriented obligations can seem to resemble merely gift giving, because the relationship invoked by the alleged obligation lacks an essential element presumed necessary for a justice relationship to exist. It is that essential reciprocity that defines justice "as fairness" (Rawls), as "mutual advantage" (Barry), or in other contractual terms that simply cannot be present in relations with future generations.

Although on one level this charge is obviously true, I want to suggest that when future generations are viewed in terms of the interests they represent, reciprocity is possible between generations, and therefore justice is as well. This is a reciprocity in the making of claims for our own and the future's interests, and it is especially prevalent when making claims (or policy) concerning the environmental interests of present and future generations. When those environmental claims are made using the language of rights – when what is

48

being claimed are the environmental human rights of future generations – then I contend that there is a reciprocal advantage gained by present generation claimants who share the same interest in protecting their environmental rights. It is a "reflexive reciprocity" – an action that rebounds on itself in furthering the interests of both present performer and future recipient. In short, protecting and furthering the environmental rights of future generations enhances and adds strength to the same rights of the present generation. Thus, respecting the rights of the future redounds to our benefit in a kind of virtual reciprocity – reflexively strengthening our rights today.

In this chapter I want to explore the possibility and acceptability of reflexive reciprocity as a foundation both for the recognition of rights and for a theory of intergenerational justice constructed around their defense. In the course of the exploration, we first must examine different conceptualizations of reciprocity and how they account for the justice relations that incorporate them. The two most prominent of these are the economic contractual models offered by Gauthier and Rawls, but a third understanding of reciprocity is also possible, one that takes into account moral sentiments and moral community as essential features of any reciprocal relationship. This third conceptualization will allow us, in the conclusion of this chapter, to reflect on the suitability of reflexive reciprocity as a suitable foundation for justice, and as a concept with which to mediate the debate between Rawls and Gauthier.

As a generator of rights, reflexive reciprocity by necessity focuses on group rights, both of present and future generations. As we shall see in the second major discussion of this chapter, this is significant within the argument for specifically *environmental* justice between generations, for two reasons. First, because future persons do not yet exist, their interests and rights can be considered only as members of a group, and it would seem, a rather abstract one as well.[1] *How* abstract within a context of nationalism and sovereign nation-states is a question for Chapter 4. Second, the justice claims of these future groups are bound up with interests that manifest the emergent quality of environmental phenomena – the interconnection of air, water, and soil. Therefore, which

---

[1] Treating future persons as members of a group only, and viewing their rights as such as group rights, is both essential to my argument and allows us to avoid getting bogged down in the abortion debate, which admittedly for some people also centers on the right of individual members of future generations to be born. The present argument about the environmental rights of future generations need not include any position whatsoever on rights to life versus women's rights to choose, unless one wants to argue that the right to choose jeopardizes the very existence of a future generation. I know of no one who would make such an extreme claim, so I will pass on. My conceptualization of the effect of present persons on those in the future will follow Derek Parfit's (1984, 387) position: "We can affect their identity. And many of our acts have this effect."

rights these future groups might claim depend for their protection both on what we do today as well as on the interactions with the environment of other future groups. In both cases, the argument for group rights takes on a unique aspect when considering environmental human rights, compared with more recent group rights arguments concerned with identity politics or minority oppression. In this chapter, we shall see how the group rights of "people like us" make environmental justice claims possible and render the whole concept of group rights more palatable.

JUSTICE, RECIPROCITY, AND MORAL SENTIMENTS

As a concept, reciprocity has been part of discussions of justice ever since Socrates first rejected his interlocutor Cephalos's suggestion, in Book I of *The Republic*, that justice consisted in "returning like for like." In this rejection Plato set the parameters for a disagreement about the nature of justice that would, after Rawls reduced justice entirely to reciprocity, become a disagreement about the nature of reciprocity. This subsequent disagreement is where we begin in a moment, but the irony of this consequence is evident in Socrates's assertion that if justice were only about reciprocity, then doing justice might result in great harm, as in returning a borrowed weapon to someone who has become deranged since the original loan. Today the same counterexample could be used as a reason to reject reciprocity as a virtue because of its contractual requirement of returning or replicating dangerous behavior. Indeed, much of the disagreement among philosophers concerning the nature of reciprocity turns on whether it is in fact a virtue or merely a relationship between two or more persons stipulating certain rules and behaviors in relation to each other.

Rawls's *Theory of Justice* (1971) argument placed reciprocity at the center of the concept of justice, and David Gauthier's *Morals by Agreement* (1986) did the same for all of morality. As we shall see in a moment, both approaches have been criticized (Barry, 1995) for misconstruing reciprocity as essentially an economic relationship having little to do with either justice or morality and too much with individual self-interest. At the other extreme are arguments by Buchanan (1990), Schumaker (1992), and Becker (1986), which place reciprocity into a virtue ethics format, making it resemble too closely personal moral inclinations or habits such as generosity, selflessness, or other "traits of character people ought to have" (Becker, 74). I shall argue that both sets of conceptualizations miss important features of reciprocity that make it recognizable in everyday life as a moral relationship that exceeds self-interested economic motivations without being altogether a matter of private moral belief or saintliness. In other words, reciprocity is a relational concept and moral sentiment denoting more than merely entering into contracts to further self-interest, but less, from a moral point of view, than selfless generosity or the giving of gifts. It is a relationship among individual people in a spirit of shared community defined by more than just economic self-interests; as such, I shall argue, it is conceivable that reciprocity can exist between present and future generations of community members. It is unlikely, however, as we shall see in Chapter 4, that this type of intergenerational communal reciprocity can easily exist between communities.

Rawls's and Gauthier's arguments are well known and need not be fully recapitulated here. They also have significant differences not only in scope – Gauthier makes reciprocity all of morality, Rawls *merely* all of justice – but also in what they presume will be the result of reciprocity between individual persons. Nevertheless, their similarities are what matter most in comparison to the virtue ethics viewpoint. For both of them, justice can be reduced to a form of reciprocity: for Gauthier the parameters of that reciprocity are defined purely by mutual self-interest; for Rawls there is an additional requirement that the reciprocity be "fair." Rawls accomplishes fairness through his ingenious rhetorical device "the original position," within which natural and social differences or inequalities between people are made irrelevant in the bargaining process because they are hidden from view by the "veil of ignorance." Nevertheless, Rawls's persons behind the veil of ignorance are motivated by the same self-interest that moves Gauthier's toward cooperation also. For neither Rawls nor Gauthier do sentiments or shared convictions enter into the hammering out of reciprocal relations between persons; all that matters to their association is the mutual benefit (defined economically) secured thereby.

Rawls's and Gauthier's understanding of reciprocity is commonly referred to as "tit for tat," and as such Brian Barry (1989) is certainly correct that future generations are left out of the reciprocal arrangements because they cannot be present in the bargaining. Rawls acknowledges this exclusion and offers the requirement of the "just savings principle" as a substitute for actual reciprocity. As many have pointed out (Barry, 1989; Beckerman and Pasek, 2001; Gibbard, 1991), however, although just savings might be admirable as a moral constraint, the principle cannot operate for Rawls with the same strength as do the two principles of justice derived from considerations of mutual self-interest.

For many commentators, the exclusions from Rawls's (and by implication Gauthier's) reciprocity-based justice do not stop with future generations, and because they do not, both renderings of reciprocity are suspect. Reciprocity as tit for tat cannot apply to future generations because persons not yet alive cannot share equal status with the living in deciding what should constitute the rules of justice. Although many philosophers, including Barry, agree with this statement, for them it is proof of the inadequacy of reciprocity as the measure of justice. Justice that manifests such exclusions simply violates common sentiments concerning what we expect from a theory of justice. The fact that even Rawls struggled mightily within his case for justice as fairness to find a place for consideration of future generations only proves the inadequacy of tit-for-tat reciprocity as a foundation for justice.

As Barry points out (1989), the problem with tit for tat is its fundamental denial of equality as the baseline for justice. Rawls's reliance on the original position and the veil of ignorance does succeed in hiding inequalities in the choice of the rules of justice, so that superior persons might not choose out of partiality, but accomplishes this not because of a shared sentiment in favor of equality. Self-interest is the motivation within the original position, and only those with ability to contribute to Rawls's "cooperative scheme for mutual advantage" are covered by the rules of justice. Clearly future generations do not qualify, but neither do many other groups. Disabled, and less intelligent or able people, as well as children, according to some accepted criteria, are also excluded from justice as tit-for-tat reciprocity. Allen Buchanan (1990, 229) argues that any view of justice that would exclude such groups clearly "clashes with commonsense morality, according to which it makes perfect sense to say that a person who is unable to contribute to the social surplus can be treated justly or unjustly, and with some of our most fundamental legal institutions, which extend basic rights to all persons, regardless of their ability to contribute."

Buchanan's often-cited argument makes clear that tit-for-tat reciprocity excludes an important aspect of the idea of justice that most people assume is essential to the concept and its rules. That aspect can be characterized a variety of ways, including some that Buchanan himself rejects that invoke too much of a virtue ethic. In general, however, a view of justice that rejects the rights of noncontributors to any share in the distribution of benefits simply sounds too harsh to be called justice. Justice as tit-for-tat reciprocity is therefore for Buchanan (p. 232) "truly a radical and severe view. In denying that noncontributors have any distributive rights at all, it rejects out of hand current debates about the extent of the rights of severely handicapped persons." Furthermore, if contribution as the measure of inclusion is construed as actual rather than potential, then "all normal children, prior to the age at which they make net contributions to the cooperative surplus, have no rights" (p. 233). In fact, Buchanan concludes that any theory of justice based on tit-for-tat reciprocity cannot consistently defend or protect human rights at all.

Buchanan's argument is telling against Rawls's and Gauthier's understanding of reciprocity, but it is still important to ask what is missing from their view that makes justice (or all of morality) based on it seem so unpalatable. The short answer is the *sentiments* of justice – attitudes and beliefs both about the content and operation of justice that go beyond notions of self-interest in creating a shared sense of collective participation in a moral life.

For Plato, it was precisely this sense of collective endeavor that made justice possible only within the political realm. Politics provided the leadership and the moral instruction that informed citizens of their place or role in the realm of justice. Modern thinkers still assume that justice is the uniquely political virtue, but not on the basis of citizen participation in a shared moral universe. Today, justice is perceived as within the political domain because it is through politics that necessary power is acquired to make distribution of valued goods both possible and, as Rawls would have it, fair. Reciprocity as tit for tat seems in this modern context both a requirement of fairness in distribution and a necessary concession to a more democratic organization of power than Plato was willing to countenance.

For critics of Rawls and the modern view of contractual justice, however, demanding a fuller concept of reciprocity need not take them all the way back to the ancient Greek understanding either of politics or of justice; our common experiences of everyday life can clearly deliver insights into what reciprocity requires and how relationships built on it often exceed the self-interest motives of tit for tat. Reciprocity can mean more than merely a shared interest in collective profit, because we know that when reciprocal relations between ourselves and others become entirely based on tit for tat, reciprocity has already been diminished as the tie that binds us in a certain type of relationship. Marriage, family, and friendship relations clearly cannot survive too stringent an insistence on tit-for-tat reciprocity. With a little self-reflection, anyone who has grown irritable waiting for a (presumed) friend to "reciprocate" with a return social invitation already understands that insisting on tit for tat has altered the basis of their friendship.

Why should reciprocity – or justice for that matter – resemble friendship? Except for Aristotle, in Books Seven and Eight of the *Ethics*, few have viewed friendship as the model for either. It would seem important, especially in response to Rawls and Gauthier, not to rely on vague moral intuitions in our rejection of justice as reciprocity. Friendship is instructive for justice, however, not necessarily because the same warmth of feeling is necessary for justice as for friendship, but because of what friends share that make friendship possible as a cooperative or reciprocal relationship.

Friendship is but one example among others of what justice requires beyond tit-for-tat reciprocity for Allan Gibbard. He recognizes (1991, 266) that all reciprocity (including that within friendship or justice) requires what he calls "terms of trade," because "we exchange unlikes, and we can ask what makes the exchange fair or unfair." Those "terms" include concepts, language, moral sentiments, and beliefs shared by all participants essential to their cooperation, because they make the positive expectations of cooperation possible. They might include a belief in the fundamental equality of all citizens, whether fit to contribute or not; they might express "common standards of fairness," or they might refer to something even more basic to human personality and interaction – friendship, respect for others as equally holders of human rights, or a sense of community. The sentiments represent the basis on which the "framework for cooperation" is constructed, and for Buchanan (p. 239), to deny that they are part of the meaning of reciprocity is to guarantee only a superficial view of justice. Without such shared sentiments and the intuitions that give rise to them, cooperation might be widely viewed and accepted as profitable, self-interested, and worthwhile, but it will not be viewed as just.

For Buchanan, when our intuition tells us that a theory of justice that would exclude children or severely disabled persons is unacceptable, we should heed our convictions that reciprocity is more than merely contractual tit for tat and that our system of justice should reflect those beliefs. Such convictions are not mere prejudices, he claims (p. 236), but are "theoretically embedded, principled practical beliefs" about the nature of reciprocity. In his view, what is lacking is a focus on participants as fellow human "subjects" deserving equal respect as ourselves, not merely potential contributors to our well-being.

Buchanan's Kantian insistence on a "subject-centered justice" changes its foundation in reciprocity by treating reciprocating participants as sharing something more than mutual self-interest; however, he does not recognize what provides the definition of Gibbard's "terms of trade" that is shared. Buchanan instead reverts to a somewhat vague "set of intuitions" about justice and reciprocity that leads persons to reject tit for tat.

Alan Gewirth (1996) and virtue theorist Lawrence C. Becker (1986) seek to flesh out the nature of Buchanan's intuitions about reciprocity, and both rely somewhat on virtue ethics to do so, although Becker far more so than Gewirth. As we have seen in Chapter 1, Gewirth locates the communal basis of human rights on the principle of mutuality: that all humans are both subjects and respondents of rights. Because they are, all humans have a reciprocal moral obligation to defend others' rights. Gewirth is careful not to fuse mutuality with reciprocity, however. They remain distinct for a variety of reasons, all but one of which make it clear that Gewirth's notion of mutuality, although it aims at full defense of human rights, is nevertheless a strictly tit-for-tat relation among persons. It is in contrasting mutuality with reciprocity that the contractual nature of Gewirth's view of reciprocity becomes clear; however, ironically, mutuality emerges as a more Buchanan-like version of reciprocity as the communal basis of human rights.

Gewirth begins to distinguish reciprocity from mutuality by making reciprocity sound more fully grounded in virtue ethics. Both mutuality and reciprocity denote dynamic and symmetrical relations between persons, but reciprocity has more to do with person A doing or returning "good" to person B. Mutuality, conversely, is more about A honoring B's rights claims and vice versa (p. 76). In the course of the discussion of mutuality's difference from reciprocity, however, Gewirth makes his tit-for-tat understanding of reciprocity clear. "The beneficiaries of reciprocity," he claims, "are limited to one's prior benefactors." Thus, as in Rawls and Gauthier, "persons are excluded from the benefits of reciprocity if they do not, or are not in a position to, confer prior benefits on other persons" (pp. 76–77). Mutuality is superior to reciprocity, Gauthier claims, because respect of others' rights is not a reaction to some prior benefit received and does not depend in other ways on prior treatment (p. 77). Instead, because of what members of a community share in terms of their beliefs about human rights, obligations to others are recognized immediately on awareness of others' existence as bearers of rights.

It is easy to see that although Gewirth has a strictly tit-for-tat understanding of reciprocity, his concept of mutuality is in fact a version of reciprocity more closely allied to Buchanan's. It is Gewirth's placing of mutuality within a communal context that renders it a more fully reciprocal concept, because the shared belief in universal human rights is the "term of trade" within which reciprocity operates in the community of rights. I shall return to and expand Gewirth's communal rewriting of the idea of reciprocity in a moment, but first it is necessary to distinguish both his view and the tit-for-tat understanding of reciprocity with that of virtue theory.

Lawrence C. Becker is clear that in his view reciprocity is a "deontic virtue" (1986, 4). This means that although like Gauthier, Becker sees all of morality as reducible to reciprocity, unlike Gauthier, reciprocity itself has far more moral content than agreement on shared interests. As a virtue theorist, Becker views the subject matter of moral theory as an exploration of "the traits of character people ought to have," rather than an investigation of what counts as a moral act or rule. Of course, chief among these traits is the capacity for reciprocity, which nevertheless Becker defines (p. 4) in terms of actions.

> The concept of reciprocity that I shall defend may be summarized in the following maxims: that we should return good for good, in proportion to what we receive; that we should resist evil, but not do evil in return; that we should make reparation for harm we do; and that we should be disposed to do those things as a matter of moral obligation.

Becker's understanding of reciprocity clearly requires more in the way of duty than does any tit-for-tat view, and in so doing fits better with Buchanan's "intuitions" about what morality requires of people. Becker's understanding relies on notions of goodness and obligation as moral sentiments that although they might be congruent with self-interest in some larger sense, they are not reducible to self-interest. These sentiments make it possible for reciprocity to manifest in Millard Schumaker's (1992) term as "sharing without reckoning."

This is possible but not probable. The problem with Becker's approach to morality in general and to reciprocity in particular is that like those of all virtue theorists, his definition of morality lies almost entirely within an individual person's own private being and set of character traits, rather than in human interaction. Whether that interaction is characterized morally in terms of a set of rules or outcomes is more or less irrelevant to Becker, because the morality of the interaction is determined by the presence of the traits supporting reciprocity, as evidenced by the participants. This is arguably a strange view of morality; it is unquestionably an even odder version of reciprocity. By its nature reciprocity must refer first to behavior – action and reaction – rather than to the traits of individual persons engaged in it. Those traits might be important in a moral sense, but if they are what define morality, then that view of morality is not about reciprocity specifically but about those traits. Becker has taken a distinctly social phenomenon and turned into a set of private motivations. He can base his moral theory on those motivations, but it is not based then on reciprocity.

What is missing in Becker's view of reciprocity is not what is lacking in Rawls and Gauthier, because he certainly brings moral sentiments to the forefront of reciprocity, whereas they see only mutual self-interest. Becker's view lacks sociality, however, the sense of collective behavior that ironically *is* present in tit for tat, even if the latter ignores essential and shared sentiments as background conditions for reciprocity to be pursued in the first place. Such a privatized view of morality as Becker's is not rare in the history of moral theory – indeed most religious views are so based – but it is difficult to escape the irony that the title of this very privatistic theory of morality is a most social word: reciprocity.

In a sense both the tit-for-tat view of reciprocity and Becker's virtue ethics characterization share the same flaw: both focus too much on the individual participants and not enough on the relation of reciprocity itself. Whereas Rawls and Gauthier stress the self-interest of each person and Becker, the private moral traits, neither get to the heart of what actually is *shared* in a relationship of reciprocity. Rawls and Gauthier focus on the outcome for each participant, and Becker on the virtue within each. Reciprocity is more than trading, however; it is about sharing. It is a distinctively social, or rather communal, event.

Several philosophers besides Plato have stressed the communal nature of reciprocity, and in so doing have distinguished a view separate from either the tit-for-tat or virtue ethics. It is within this understanding of reciprocity as sharing and mutual concern between members of what Golding (1981, 64) calls a "moral community" that the possibility arises for reciprocity between generations. In the remainder of this section I shall sketch this view of communal reciprocity; in the next section I shall explore its transformation into reflexive reciprocity within a "cross-generational" or "transgenerational community" (Baier, 1981; de-Shalit, 1995).

Communitarian theorist Michael Sandel echoes Buchanan's insistence that reciprocity includes moral sentiments and beliefs about goodness. These traits make up what are shared by members of a community that is itself "constitutive" of personal identity in the sense of providing a strong sense of shared identity as well. Such communities and the reciprocity evident within them are not merely contractual in nature, Sandel argues, because "reciprocity points through the contract to an antecedent moral requirement" shared by all members (p. 107). All members must agree on an "independent moral principle" of fairness that makes reciprocity possible, and this sharing of belief both defines their community and its individual members and makes reciprocity prevalent in their lives. Following Sandel, Schumaker then likens reciprocity to a "covenant" that establishes a society as a moral community, rather than the old metaphor of social contract. As in Sandel, the difference lies in what participants share *before* the contract: "mutual esteem and concern, friendship, general affection, and concern for one's partner" (pp. 35, 36). Without these elements reciprocity loses its essential meaning as "sharing without reckoning" that distinguishes it, in Schumaker's view, from the merely contractual relations underlying justice and reciprocity as conceived by Hume and his contemporary inheritors Rawls and Gauthier.

Sandel and Schumaker together locate the moral sentiments and beliefs on which human reciprocity relies within communities, and it is only as members of communities, therefore, that real reciprocity is possible. Without a shared sense of fairness or fair play, reciprocity is merely contractual tit for tat (de-Shalit, p. 96), but unlike Becker, Sandel and Schumaker insist that such constitutive moral beliefs are not private character traits but socially agreed-on ties that bind individual persons into community and in the process give them a moral identity.

This communal understanding of reciprocity is one that fits well with our intuitions about the meaning of reciprocal relations precisely because it does not envision the exclusionary consequences of Rawls's and Gauthier's tit-for-tat relations. People in community cannot tolerate such results because as members of a community they are defined by how they treat each other and how they allow all their compatriots to be treated. Exclusionary reciprocity (tit for tat) would be viewed as bigotry or unwelcome discrimination. It is only within community that real reciprocity, and therefore real justice, is possible. Significantly, in his later books, *Political Liberalism* (1993) and *The Law of Peoples* (1999), Rawls himself comes to recognize the importance for justice of a shared identity that comes from political institutions and cultural factors rather than merely the dictates of private self-interest. Private self-interest can exist anywhere that people do; reciprocity, or at least the kind that underwrites justice, prevails only within the domain of community.

REFLEXIVE RECIPROCITY AND CROSS-GENERATIONAL COMMUNITIES

Communities, of course, encompass many generations of members, as Edmund Burke was the first modern thinker to remark. For Burke (1910, 143, 144), community represents a partnership whose ends "cannot be obtained in many generations," and so "it becomes a partnership not only between those who are living, but between those who are living, those who are dead, and those who are to be born." As we saw in Chapter 1, like Burke's, Avner de-Shalit's concept of transgenerational community incorporates not only past generations into a community's sense of itself but also future generations. De-Shalit's argument proceeds on the grounds that part of what is shared within a strongly communal association is a sense of collective identity, an identity that can only be "constitutive" of individual identity as a member if it includes consideration of future members.

If reciprocity is a defining characteristic of justice between individual members in a community, then we must ask what present generations know or can assume about future members for reciprocity to be possible with them. I answer that we know two important things about future generations of our community. First, we know which things they will hold as important moral and communal values because we share them as well, and we presume that those values will continue to be contained within political institutions and social practices that reflect those of our own time. Second, we know which essential – Barry (1999, 99) would say "vital" – interests they share with each other and with us. Those interests, because they are fundamental in nature, generate rights both for ourselves and our future generations.

Annette Baier (1981, 174) points out that when considering the "moral tie between us and future generations," it is crucial to recognize that the only unique element in this relationship compared with those with the living "lies in the inferiority of our knowledge about them, not in the inferiority of their ontological status." An important aspect of that status is the attribution of interests to future persons. Baier argues that though our knowledge about them is clearly limited, we can recognize that whichever interests they will have are linked with ours in a relationship of interdependency, and that "rights and duties attach to roles in a network of interdependent roles" (179). She therefore concludes that mutual interests of present and future generations should result in recognition of the human rights of future persons.

Baier's argument is supportive of my own, but its success relies on whether the identifiable interests of future generations qualify as essential enough to generate rights. Feinberg's (1980a, 182) well-known discussion of such interests ends with his conclusion that although the future's interests "cry out for protection from invasions that can take place now," they are not as yet "actual" interests, and therefore protection of them cannot qualify as a rights-induced duty for the living. No one can assume the existence of any particular set of future persons, therefore "[N]o one can complain on behalf of presently nonexistent future generations that their future interests, which give them a contingent right of protection, have been violated since they will never come into existence to be wronged" (p. 182). Feinberg's specific example in this argument is the imaginary decision by all living persons not to reproduce, but his conclusion applies to all future persons as specific persons because no single one of them has a right to be born and therefore presents no "actual" rights.

Baier's assertion that the ontological status of future generations is not germane to the question of their rights runs counter to Feinberg's conclusion that the future cannot be said to possess rights against the living, but there is a better way to respond to Feinberg, which focuses not on the holder of interests either now or in the future but on the interests themselves. The interests with which we are concerned in the attribution of environmental rights are those of the living and not yet born to clean air, water, and soil. We have already seen that they qualify as essential interests, but, contrary to Feinberg, we need also to recognize that they are not merely the potential interests of potential people but "actual" interests in the fullest sense.

Consider then that these are interests that by their very nature unite present and future in important ways. They exist, as it were, simultaneously now *and* in the future in one and the same time. They characterize our condition *and* the condition of future people. Their protection is essential to our welfare *and* to the welfare of later generations. It is the very interconnection of the present and future interests that characterizes environmental goals *as* interests. We cannot protect the future's interests in environmental quality without simultaneously also protecting our own, and we cannot protect our own without protecting the future's. Our action therefore in protecting these interests is not only a duty to the future but also reverberates back on our own interests to protect them. In other words, if we recognize the environmental interests of the future as actual interests that we also share as equally basic to us, then our protection of them reciprocally protects our own interests.

Furthermore, because they are vital or "basic" interests, their connection to rights is already established. If the interests themselves unite present and future holders in a shared stake in the same goal, then our rights, it seems, must be similarly wedded together. Our environmental interests are in a relationship of reciprocity with the environmental interests of the future.

I should like to call this a "reflexive reciprocity," because only the present agents carrying the future's environmental interests actually exist; future generations will add additional agents. This "virtuality" does not vitiate the real reciprocating effect of the future's interests, however. Furthermore, environmental interests are unique in this relationship with the future, and different from other interests also protected by rights. For instance, someone might argue that all rights represent interests for which we desire future protection as well, for example, the rights to free speech or religion.

I think that a little reflection, however, will elucidate why environmental rights carry a special reciprocity when compared with other types of rights. As much as we might defend the future's interests in free speech or religion, our own liberty does not depend on guaranteeing the same liberty for future persons. We could, in other words, simultaneously protect our freedom of speech while saying that this right will expire with our own generation. As reprehensibly irresponsible as such a course might be in terms of being good stewards of our freedoms, it nevertheless would not necessarily diminish our liberty to exercise our rights. Our liberty is not enhanced by protecting the future's liberty in these areas, but our air, water, and soil *are* enhanced by our protecting those elements for future generations to enjoy as well. Protecting the environmental interests of the future requires that we start doing so now, and cleaning the air, water, and soil now benefits our interests as well.

Even if we recognize the actual, essential, and reciprocating interests of the future in a healthy environment, does it follow then to say that we are speaking of actual moral rights that future generations hold, the protection of which binds us then into a relationship of intergenerational justice? We have so far argued that the essential nature of the interests is enough to warrant the rights attached to them, but I think that an additional argument is needed concerning the status of future generations as members of our moral community that can therefore hold rights that we are duty-bound to recognize.

The concept of human rights, of course, posits a moral community of all persons, within which all are entitled to equal consideration as a matter of human dignity. Baier takes this to mean that if the ontological status of all future persons is no different than that of the living, then as members of our moral community they also should be seen as rights holders. This works logically to grant immediately to all future persons rights equal to my own, but this seems to me to stretch the idea of a moral community too far in the service of a universalistic interpretation of human rights. It replaces the future generations (with their interests and rights) of my own community with the future generations of all people in all communities everywhere, no matter how different culturally they are to me, and even including those from cultures who deny the whole idea of human rights. Although admittedly their environmental interests would be well served by my viewing them as rights-based claims on my own environmental obligations, it is probably difficult for *me* to see them as such claims, because my moral community seems much smaller.

As we have seen, theorists of community recognize that a moral community is one that constitutes a sense of shared identity based on shared values, beliefs, and moral principles. Such communities invariably rely on a deep reverence for their own histories and for the former citizens who populate them and who passed on those values, beliefs, and principles to the living. Baier argues that reverence for the past is predicated on no less a belief in the ontological status of those forbears than on those who come after us; therefore, what we owe as a matter of right to the past we also must preserve as a matter of right for the future. We are merely the current occupants of a "cross-generational moral community."

> The crucial role we fill, as moral beings, is as members of a cross-generational community, a community of beings who look before and after, who interpret the past in the light of the present, who see the future as growing out of the past, who see themselves as members of enduring families, nations, cultures, traditions. (p. 177)

Because we share the same space of those from the past and future, a space defined by our shared institutions, customs, and principles, we recognize the rights of both as engaging our reciprocal (and reciprocating) duties.

Baier here cannot be speaking of the community of all human beings in all communities – living, dead, and not yet born. Human rights theory might postulate such a community borderless in either space or time, but as we shall see in Chapter 4, both communitarian theorists and our own moral intuitions do not agree. We recognize those generations before and after us as members of our moral community only if they occupy a space defined by the same institutions, customs, and principles as our own. In other words, they are "people like us" in important ways in which others do not qualify. All communities partly define themselves by those who do not belong as well as by those who do.

We know what past and future members of our community did and will believe morally and politically because we believe it too, whereas those from other nations or cultural communities might not; we are indebted to our communal predecessors for our beliefs, and we take care to protect those beliefs for our inheritors. We must know that we are people of the same beliefs to include them in our moral community and therefore to honor and protect their rights. Our recognition of those rights depends on our recognition of future citizens as part of "us"; if we cannot recognize them as members of our moral community who share our identity, we cannot recognize their rights. In this sense it must be said that when it comes to the recognition of rights and duties across generations, "all human rights are local."

This might seem an oddly parochial conclusion to an argument concerning intergenerational justice grounded on the rights to such global and interconnected phenomena as clean air, water, and soil, but a community-based understanding of rights capable of extending to future generations cannot make any claim on present generations greater than that owed to future members of their own community. Nevertheless, as I have stated before, it is the universal capacity of all cultures and communities to be concerned with the rights of their own successor generations that allows the possibility of a truly universal notion of the human rights of those generations. Environmental human rights then offer a new foundation for a truly cross-cultural consensus on human rights by raising the consciousness of each community to its obligations to the future. Environmental rights awareness accomplishes this by focusing each community's attention on its *own* successor generations and their environmental rights, and on how doing so reciprocally benefits the present generation.

This reciprocity of environmental rights and interests across generations also makes what I call reflexive reciprocity interestingly tit for tat, at the same time it is clearly a communally based notion that is not exclusionary, in the way of Rawls or Gauthier. The concept of reflexive reciprocity therefore manages to bring together both sides of the argument over the meaning of reciprocity discussed earlier in this chapter, including both the grounding in shared beliefs and mutual concern characterized by the notion of community while also improving, in good tit-for-tat manner, the interests and prospects of the reciprocating partners – present and future generations.

Reflexive reciprocity accomplishes this theoretical synthesis by postulating rights of the future that are distinctly collective in nature – the group rights of future generations. Environmental human rights are distinctively group rights because of the communally based relationship of reciprocity that they establish between generations. After all, future generations can be perceived ontologically only as groups because no specific persons yet exist. Still, environmental rights present a different aspect from other so-called group rights as they have been discussed in human rights literature thus far. It is this aspect that remains to be explored as part of the argument for an intergenerational environmental justice based on the reciprocity relations existing between present and future human rights.

ENVIRONMENTAL RIGHTS AND JUSTICE BETWEEN PRESENT AND FUTURE GROUPS

Because emergent environmental rights invoke images of the rights of those who come after us, it might be concluded that these rights are particularly individualist in their universal application. On the contrary, however, emergent rights need to be viewed primarily as group rights, as controversial as that concept still remains. I cannot address the entire dispute concerning group rights as it has been engaged by Crawford (1988), Kymlicka (1995 a, b), Rawls (1999), and Young (1990; 2000), among many others, but nevertheless, both the communal and emergent character of environmental human rights adds an interesting and different twist on the argument sustaining group rights.

Employing human rights to guarantee environmental interests of future generations would seem also to rely on an especially abstract notion of groups who have rights, because the groups do not yet exist. Because the persons who will fill these groups are obviously indeterminate, if indeed they can be said to have rights it is obvious that they do so only as members of the group defined as a set of future persons (Weiss, 1989, 96). In an important sense, however, future citizens as a group are less abstract in the eyes of present generations than even groups that exist today in other cultures. Because they represent the future of our own society, their identity is somewhat known to us even though obviously as individual people we have no relationship with them, but they are *our* future generations who will continue many of the political, institutional, and cultural practices and artifacts that define us today as a community and as individual people. To some extent, therefore, they are recognizable concretely in their similarity as "part of us."

Most group rights arguments are intrinsically about the role of identity and community within the minds of people who identify with a particular group, whether defined in terms of ethnicity, language, religion, or particular history. Although Young (2000, 82ff) warns that group identity as "difference" should be seen in terms of relations rather than substance to avoid reifying the idea of group identity, it is still the case that group rights arguments proceed as minority claims to recognition of difference from the majority or (usually) the more powerful groups in society. For instance, it is in this interpretation, that Kymlicka (1989) argues that the culture rights of indigenous minorities be granted as a kind of compensatory justice for the inequality of power that characterizes their position in society.

If group rights are granted on the basis of the value of protecting cultural difference, as Kymlicka argues, then it is important to recognize, as Young (2000, 91) does, that "cultural difference emerges from internal and external relations. People discover themselves with cultural affinities that solidify them into groups by virtue of their encounter with those who are culturally different in some or many respects." The key for Young is the idea of relationship, rather than acceptance of particular features of members of the group, such as race, language, or history, that sets them apart as "different." Young's argument is an important one and somewhat accepted by Kymlicka (1996, 24) in his characterization of the two human rights claimed by indigenous groups: the right of "internal restriction" and the right of "external protections."

Both of these rights call attention to the relationships that define the internal workings of the group and its difference from larger society. Thus, they avoid the reification that Young cautions against. In so doing they also manage to avoid most of the pitfalls of the "identity politics" or "politics of recognition" that have occupied both contemporary politics and political theorists. (See Elshtain, 1995, Taylor, 1992, and Gutmann and Thompson, 1996.) Kymlicka's call to recognize the value for all of society in recognizing the group cultural rights of indigenous groups both protects such groups but also acknowledges their place (or, for Young, their "relationship") with the collective identity of the larger society.

What Young and Kymlicka provide for my argument is the recognition that groups rights do not protect an ossified group identity from external influence as much as they serve both cultures in relationship with each other. This relationship moves both groups continually to reassess and redefine their own identities and that of their members. In so doing, the rights of each group to its historic culture as well as the human rights of each individual member are both protected. In the same way the recognition of the rights that future generations as a group have to environmental goods over which we have current control serves to solidify our relationship with those future groups. It is a relationship of reciprocity not only of interests (as we have seen) but also of reciprocal *identities*.

Future generations of our community share as a group our identity through the relationship we both have with the same cultural traditions, beliefs, and practices that define us both as members of the same moral community. As such we constitute with them what David Miller (1995) calls a "community of obligation." We shall explore the strength and exclusivity of that obligation in the next chapter, but it is worth noting here that another element of reciprocity with future generations is evident in recognizing our obligation to further their environmental human rights. In doing so we pass on cultural artifacts that define our relationship with the environment and have become part of our identity as a national culture. In our anticipation of the environmental benefits for our inheritors we secure our connection with them as a group that shares our identity.

Few question the role of past generations in providing the group or national identity of present groups, and it is common to acknowledge obligations or debts of gratitude to those who went before in appreciation of their sacrifices and their general contributions to defining our identity. Such obligations are real because they identify us as a people; that is why we acknowledge and accept them – not to do so would entail a denial of who we are. For that reason too we do not expect other countries or their citizens to accept the same obligations, but our anticipation of successor generations of our nation plays the same role in the maintenance of our cultural identity, and our obligations to them are equally as real. To deny this, as Annette Baier (1981, 182) concludes, would be to deny all obligation as mere superstition, for as Martin Golding (1972, 91 [*Obligations to Future Generations*, **Monist**, January]) insists, "if obligation to the past is superstition, then so is obligation to the future." It is in our acceptance of both that our identity as a group is secured. Securing the human rights for future generations – including environmental rights – not only is in our interests then, because they are reciprocally served by those of the future; it is also how we define ourselves as a nation with the reciprocal aid of those who come after us.

CONCLUSION: THE RECIPROCATING FUTURE

I have argued in this chapter that inasmuch as justice presumes reciprocity, then reciprocity must manifest two distinct elements. First, it must be more than mere "tit for tat" economic exchange; rather, reciprocity must encompass what Gibbard calls the "terms of trade" that Rawls in *The Law of Peoples* (1999) recognizes are definitive cultural artifacts that citizens share both with their predecessors and successors. Second, reciprocity therefore is intrinsically a part of communal living, and community identity is itself a product of such reciprocity. If these two arguments concerning reciprocity are valid, then the idea of reciprocity with the future as a feature of intergenerational environmental justice based on human rights is not difficult to grasp.

Communities presume their own cross-generational existence as they revere their pasts and attempt to guarantee their futures. It is in the values that it shares with its past and anticipates passing on to its inheritors that a community's past, present, and future interests become evident, and within which communal arguments can be made for protecting those interests as a matter of human right.

This dynamic of reciprocal preserving and sustaining of essential interests and communal identity is, I would argue, what makes justice possible in any society, but is especially prevalent in the case of environmental justice. I shall close this chapter's argument by suggesting two further points about the reciprocity that underlies justice across generations. The first is, as just mentioned, that nowhere is this reciprocity more in evidence – and more necessary – than in the area of environmental protection. Second, and somewhat ironically given the first point, this reciprocity does not extend to all future generations but only to those of our own society.

The interconnection of modern life is never more apparent nor better understood than in the context of environmental degradation and the need for preservation. Our natural environment is the singular physical manifestation of our connectedness both with our contemporaries and also with those who in their own future will inherit our space, our land, our air, water, and soil. The buildings that we build will crumble or be razed; our technology will be exceeded and replaced, but what we leave buried in the ground, submerged in waters, or floating in the air will constitute a physical legacy alongside the cultural legacy of our communal life. Our successors are surely at our mercy to preserve our (and therefore their) physical environment, but we are also at the mercy of our own capacity to honor *their* human right to clean air, water, and soil. If we do not do so we harm ourselves as well. We depend on their environmental human rights to make as strong a case as possible for our own; that, it seems to me, is a degree of interconnection that makes our reciprocal dependence clear, and intergenerational environmental justice possible.

For both practical and philosophical reasons, however, we should be careful not to broaden too far the scope of intergenerational reciprocity and therefore environmental justice. It is the richness of our interconnection, not merely our physical interdependence, that gives rise to our obligation to respect the environmental human rights of future generations. This is a subtle distinction perhaps, but an important one nevertheless in terms of how achievable the goal of environmental preservation based on human rights is to become. If all that we share with future generations is our dependence on a clean environment and our related reciprocal rights and duties, then there is no reason to distinguish between the future generations of my own society and those of all others. Indeed, as Baier (1981, 179) concludes, "the cross-temporal community in which one finds oneself is not restricted to those who share one's own way of life, but extends to all those with whom one stands, directly or indirectly, in dependency or interdependency relations." If she is right, then my communal ties with future generations of my own community are no stronger than with those of all societies, especially in light of the environmental interconnection that spans the entire globe regardless of national or cultural borders. Instead, "the tie linking those who are living, those who are dead, and those who are yet to be born is a cross-cultural one and brings it about that (at least) no one human is alien to me" (Baier, p. 179).

Baier surely goes too far in the name of the "rights of future persons," however. Environmentally speaking, it is true that all future generations are dependent on decisions that we make today in our society concerning the air, water, and soil, but we are not *reciprocally* dependent on the rights of any future generations other than those of our own society. Our arguments today for environmental preservation are enhanced by the rights of our own inheritors, but not those of all societies. This is the special, "reflexive" reciprocity that I have argued for here, and it exists only within cultures across their own generations. Why is this so? Because interconnection of the type I am elucidating includes more than physical interdependence, although admittedly physical interdependency might underwrite an argument for tit-for-tat reciprocity with all future persons who share my interests.

The interconnection of which I speak includes cultural continuity and the passing on of political institutions that mark a community as continuing *as a community* over the passage of time. We must identify with and care enough for those who come after us to recognize our obligations to them and their interests as possessing the power of actual rights. Without such a connection, we might indeed acknowledge either a tit-for-tat reciprocity of interests with all future persons or a supererogatory obligation to them to pass on a healthy environment, but we could never elevate it to the level of the human right of the future to demand this of us, and it is this elevation that reflexive reciprocity depends on as an argument for environmental justice.

The next chapter takes up this complex and difficult argument by recognizing it as an essentially political one. The universality of the whole idea of rights as "human" rights would seem to militate against my position, even if its pragmatic appeal is granted. Nevertheless, reflexive reciprocity need not therefore be merely a parochial idea or responsibility that serves to separate communities as they look out for the human rights of only their own future citizens. It can still lead to a global consensus on the human right to a healthy environment by relying on the care that all societies extend to their own future generations. As David Hume first recognized, however, moral agreement and concern are possible only within communities; between communities agreement – even of a moral sort – is a matter of politics.

4

Cosmopolitan Ethics, Communal Reciprocity, and Global Environmentalism

If the world is to contain a public space, it cannot be erected for one generation and planned for the living only; it must transcend the life-span of mortal men.

Hannah Arendt, *The Human Condition*

In the last chapter I argued that the requirement of reciprocity as an element of justice rendered justice possible only within a community that is characterized by a set of both shared interests and moral beliefs. I concluded by arguing that when applied to environmental justice, this means that communities are in a relationship of reciprocity with only their own future generations and not with all future persons. This less-than-cosmopolitan requirement of reciprocity has both moral and political significance, especially because, as we saw Brian Barry argue in Chapter 1, it raises the possibility that moral communities will ignore the welfare of other future communities to which one's own community's successor generations will not belong. In moral terms this possibility appears to allow too unacceptable levels of preferential treatment (even if reciprocal) for it to be associated with the concept of justice; in political terms it seems to lionize nationalism at its worst.

To avoid such dismal conclusions, we should first recognize that both moral philosophy and political theory have long histories of considering the place of "moral particularism" (as philosophers refer to preference for compatriots) and of nationalism within the realm of justice. Partly these histories reflect the presence of the concept (and often the goal) of human community as foundational both of morality and politics. Today, however, globalization threatens both foundations by its ability to eradicate borders between nations and spaces between individual persons in a world made smaller by modern communication technologies. Globalization even affects the philosophical debate itself, in that it is sometimes called an argument between moral parochialism versus cosmopolitanism, although it should be pointed out that advocates of the latter rather exclusively employ such terminology. In a globalized world, who wants to think of oneself as parochial?

There is at least irony then in my construal of environmental human rights as requiring a particularistic, even nationalistic, form of reciprocity as the basis of justice, because neither environmentalism nor certainly globalization appear amenable to such a narrowed focus. It should be remembered, however, that my argument is *not* that current generations should recognize a broad or unspecified *moral* obligation to be concerned about the environmental welfare of future generations, nor that what is required is a *political* obligation to world order in some inclusive sense covering the global natural environment. I am arguing specifically for a human right that future generations should be recognized as possessing, in this case, to clean air, water, and soil. The realm of rights, especially human rights, is characterized not just morally or politically, but legally.

In law, human rights are creatures of national governments, as is often commented on, because they are both protected and potentially violated predominantly at that level. James Nickel (2002, 358) states that "one's own country remains the main addressee of one's human rights, and one's legal system remains the primary forum for dealing with alleged violations of one's rights." Historically, and beginning in 1945 with the Universal Declaration of Human Rights (UDHR), this legal orientation toward national governments has been explicit and sustained within the human rights regime and evident in virtually all human rights declarations and agreements.[1] Therefore, any human right, environmental or otherwise, is always operative mainly at the national level in the legal sense, even if morally or politically the language used to characterize it is more universal or at least global in scope. For the foreseeable future then, environmental rights will at least be implemented and enforced by separate national governments for their own (and future) citizens. This does not rule out international agreements of course, and we shall explore several of them in Chapter 6, but the fate of the Kyoto Protocol makes clear that at the end of the day, internationally recognized human rights always depend on acceptance within national communities.

Chapter 6 explores more fully the legal consequences of environmental human rights within a broad discussion of their implementation. Here I note

---

[1] These include **The African Charter on Human and Peoples' Rights, Convention on the Prevention and Punishment of the Crime of Genocide, Convention on the Elimination of All Forms of Discrimination Against Women, The International Covenant on Civil and Political Rights, The International Covenant on Economic, Social and Cultural Rights, The European Convention on Human Rights and Fundamental Freedoms,** and **The Universal Declaration of Human Rights.**

them mostly to establish at least a prima facie case for why a communally defined reciprocity underlying environmental human rights and justice should not be summarily ruled out. Of course, an immediate issue arises about whether it is legitimate to consider nations actual communities in the moral sense, even if they clearly are legal communities. There are also larger issues that need exploration and resolution before we can decide on the appeal of environmental human rights, and these issues are the topics of this chapter.

The first topic invokes the debate between moral philosophers concerning what has become known as moral cosmopolitanism versus moral particularism (sometimes "parochialism"). Within modern philosophy, the latter was initially associated with David Hume, whose well-known skepticism about the power of reason to cause people to act morally led him to challenge the persuasiveness and efficacy of natural law as well. For Hume, moral behavior relied on sentiments like sympathy to move people into action. Sympathy exists as a human trait because of reason, Hume acknowledged, but it notoriously ebbed as distance increased. Because of sympathy's limitations, most persons were "partial" or more concerned morally with persons closest to them; therefore particular obligations to family, friends, and fellow citizens properly took moral precedence in Hume's eyes over those to more distant persons.

Conversely, moral cosmopolitanism asserts universal standards of ethical obligation and treatment of others regardless of their relationship to us. Kant is most associated with this position, and it is his retrieval of the moral efficacy of reason from Humean skepticism that is often credited with making modern natural law resistant to utilitarian critique and also therefore capable of laying the foundation for human rights. During the seventeenth century, moral cosmopolitanism became the liberal argument both for liberal world government in Condorcet, as well as the genteel anarchism of William Godwin. Godwin's example of refusing to give moral priority to the emergency needs of his mother over those of Archbishop Fenelon, a famous philanthropist with whom he was not acquainted, set the tone for utilitarianism based on moral cosmopolitanism and probably also set the stage for twentieth-century critiques of cosmopolitanism as relying too heavily on abstraction in recognizing obligations to others.

Moral cosmopolitanism embraces both utilitarian and human rights approaches to morality, because both are universal in the sense that moral behavior is to be guided by adherence to either one general moral principle (utility) or a set of them (natural law and human rights). Furthermore, cosmopolitanism insists that the application of these rules be the same in all cases of moral choice, regardless of "particularist" considerations such as kinship, closeness, or emotional attachment to the recipient of aid or concern. The debate between moral cosmopolitanism and particularism is clearly relevant to environmental human rights as I have construed them, because my communally based environmental right falls within the particularist camp, and does so almost counterintuitively given the universalist nature of human rights, and the clearly cosmopolitan (or global) character of the natural environment.

The second general topic of the present chapter centers on the moral status of the concept and practice of nationalism. Up to this point I have construed the transgenerational moral obligation to respect environmental rights as one grounded in shared communal identity and responsibility. Given that the recognition of these obligations inevitably must be incorporated in the legal codes of nations if they are to have status as human rights, the question naturally arises whether nations are properly viewed as moral communities capable of encompassing the obligations entailed by such rights of future citizens.

Beyond this initial concern with nationalism, however, lies a broader issue of whether nationalism, once compared by Einstein to "other infantile diseases like measles," is more accurately viewed in general as antagonistic to all moral systems and behavior, including those based on human rights. The cosmopolitanism/particularist debate is clearly invoked here as well, because nationalism presumes moral preference for one's fellow citizens at least, if not also for the nation as a whole as "fatherland," or the more current "homeland." Given the widely divergent environmental records across even developed nations today, it is certainly questionable whether nationalism is a help or hindrance to the argument for environmental human rights. The work of David Miller (1988, 1995), Yael Tamir (1993), and Margaret Moore (2001), among many others, has resuscitated a lively debate about nationalism today and its role in moral and political life. Exploring this argument as well as the prior one into moral cosmopolitanism/particularism will bring us at the end of this chapter to an appreciation (at least) of how environmental human rights can make concrete and pressingly real large areas of moral and political philosophy.

MORAL PARTICULARISM AND ENVIRONMENTAL HUMAN RIGHTS

All human rights would seem to presume a universalistic understanding that each and every human being has the same rights, simply, as Donnelly (1989, 12) says, "because one is a human being." Therefore, if future generations have environmental rights in my eyes only if they are of "my" community, this would be an obvious violation of the universal nature of human rights. A commitment to human rights would seem then to obviate much of the debate among moral philosophers over the acceptability of particular moral obligation to some persons but not to others, that is, to give moral preference to those closest to us. If, as human rights theory claims, all persons are equally endowed with human rights, then our concomitant duties should also be owed equally to all humans, not just to some and not just to those closest to us.

Two general objections to the human rights resolution in favor of moral universalism (often termed "cosmopolitanism" by its defenders) arise rather immediately. First, even if we all agreed that human rights are valid and that therefore all humans are equally entitled to them *and* to the duties that they entail, these rights by themselves might not rule out additional, special moral obligations due to some particular persons or groups of persons. The reason is simple: human rights might not exhaust the total of all ethical obligations or entitlements. Honoring obligations owed to others on the basis of their human rights might therefore still leave some areas of life uncovered in ethical terms and subject to other, non–rights-based obligations.

Second and related to the first, to say that the existence of human rights makes our moral obligations to all persons clear ignores important complications and nuances in human identity caused by the rich variation in human relationships. Chapter 2 showed that individual identity is affected mightily, perhaps causally, by those relationships. Our relationships with others constitute who we are. The obligations to others to which these relationships give rise might be of the non–rights-based variety mentioned previously; therefore, our own identities to some extent depend on the special, non–rights-based obligations that we owe to others. Those obligations will not be universalizable in the sense that they are owed to every other person equally, because we are not the spouse or lover of every other person, or the sister of every other person, or the teammate, fellow parishioner, or even fellow citizen of every other person. Our relations with each of them might incur both rights and obligations, but of a more specific, less universal variety than human rights and the obligations such rights levy on us all.

The mere fact of human rights therefore does not by itself resolve the issue in the moral particularism/moral universalism debate. Because the full parameters of all human relations are not defined either by human rights or the obligations they entail, even if we were to agree that all persons universally are due our equal consideration for the furtherance of their human rights, they might still not be worthy of equal consideration in other areas. My argument for environmental human rights is somewhat more modest than this, however. I shall argue that we are entitled morally to be *more* concerned with the human rights of some future persons than with those of others, and that our preferred future subjects are the future generations of our own moral community. In the latter part of this chapter I shall also argue for why that moral community should be seen as the nation.

Another way to construe this differential level of concern is to say that I am morally required to respond only to the environmental human rights held by the future successors of my own community (i.e., nation), not to those of all future persons. To make this argument we must locate it more fully within the larger discussion of moral particularism/universalism.

MORAL PARTICULARISM VERSUS MORAL UNIVERSALISM

The classic statements of the opposition between particularism and universalism are found in the following two passages from Hume and Kant. In the first, Hume establishes the particularist approach that Henry Shue identifies as "concentric circles of outwardly diminishing responsibility" (1980, 134). The second, from Kant's *Foundations of the Metaphysics of Morals*, professes Kant's faith in the ability of reason alone to overcome the partiality implicit in what he considered the sentimentality of Hume's approach to moral responsibility. In the *Treatise* (1896, 448), Hume states:

> Now it appears, that in the original frame of our mind, our strongest attention is confin'd to ourselves; our net is extended to our relations and acquaintance; and 'tis only the weakest which reaches to strangers and indifferent persons. This partiality, then, and unequal affection, must not only have an influence on our behavior and conduct in society, but even on our ideas of vice and virtue; so as to make us regard any remarkable transgression of such a degree of partiality, either by too great an enlargement, or contraction of the affections, as vicious and immoral.

In defense of universal reason, Kant (1959, 410–411) responds:

> For the pure conception of duty and of the moral law generally, with no admixture of empirical inducements, has an influence on the human heart so much more powerful than all other incentives which may be derived from the empirical field that reason, in the consciousness of its dignity, despises them and gradually becomes master over them.

Kant's last clause in this quotation effectively draws the battle lines between particularists and universalists over the relative importance of sentiments or reason in generating moral obligations and their acceptance. This basic disagreement continues today, as David Miller (1995, 58) summarizes, "the [Kantian] universalist sees in particularism a failure of rationality; the [Humean] particularist sees in universalism a commitment to abstract rationality that exceeds the capacities of ordinary human beings." When it comes to human rights, the Kantian declares that every other person is equally due my consideration of what each is due, and we would extend this to future persons also to protect their rights. The Humean particularist would scoff at such an abstract embrace of equal consideration and simply say that no real person is capable of that degree of caring about other people's rights. To care about their rights, we must know them at least a little and care about them as persons somehow important to us.

Universalism today is not restricted to Kantians who base morality on duty and rationality-based adherence to universal rules, because utilitarians are also universalists. Both agree, however, that adherence to some universal rule that should be applied equally in all cases, whether one is considering obligations to a close relative or someone on the other side of the globe, is what characterizes moral behavior.

Particularists see such abstract equality as beyond the abilities of human beings to ignore either their surroundings or their feelings about the persons close to them. Hume went so far, of course, as to claim that reason could by itself move no one to action on behalf of another; it needed the spur of passion, that is, of emotional attachment, or in his terms, of "sympathy." Particularists today do not always denigrate reason's efficacy so roundly but nevertheless insist that the power of sentimental attachment cannot be ignored in how people can and should approach their moral obligations to others. For feminists that attachment is called "care," for proto-Marxists it is a shared consciousness, for patriots it is called citizenship, and for communitarians it is a shared "rootedness and identity." To deny these very human attachments, Alasdair MacIntyre (1984, 12) famously argues:

> [R]equires of me to assume an abstract and artificial – perhaps even an impossible – stance, that of a rational being as such, responding to the requirements of morality not qua parent or farmer or quarterback, but qua rational agent who has abstracted him or herself from all social particularity, who has become not merely Adam Smith's impartial spectator, but a correspondingly impartial actor, and one who in his impartiality is doomed to rootlessness, to be a citizen of nowhere. How can I justify to myself performing this act of abstraction and detachment?

Although MacIntyre here conflates the two, particularism is not the same as partiality, even though universalists often accuse particularists of violating the basic ethical principle of impartiality. The widespread criticism of Rawls's (1999) *The Law of Peoples* as anticosmopolitan is a good case in point, although what Rawls means by a "people" and how it differs from a nation state is a topic for the next section.[2] Miller (1995, 54) points out, however, that as it applies

---

[2] A good recent collection of critical essays on Rawls's book is Rex Martin and David A. Reidy (2006), **Rawls's Law of Peoples: A Realistic Utopia?** Malden, MA: Blackwell. Part II deals specifically with Rawls's alleged partiality and anticosmopolitanism.

to moral theory and behavior, partiality "means treating someone (possibly yourself) favourably in defiance of ethically sanctioned rules and procedures," and as such is clearly unethical. MacIntyre is nevertheless accurately portraying himself as a particularist, who therefore does indeed make distinctions in his ethical relations with others and does so on the basis not of reason but because of his different relationships with them. This treatment is not always equal, but it is wrong to therefore call it partial, in the particularist view, because different rules cover the treatment in different cases. Particularists apply moral rules just as universalists do; they just believe that different rules apply in different instances, therefore, as Miller concludes, "they simply deny that impartiality consists in taking up a universalist perspective."

In other words, particularists believe that different relationships require different degrees of attention to the welfare of the persons with whom they are related, and that these different degrees of concern are determined largely by how intense the relationship is. Rather than reason, it is sentiments such as care, love, or mutual identification – and their intensity – that determine the level of moral commitment for particularists. They are equally appalled by Godwin's preference for the welfare of a famously good – although unknown to him – archbishop over that of his mother as they are by utilitarian Peter Singer's (1975) recommendation of equal treatment for animals and human infants.

Following Hume, particularists today, whether feminists, communitarians, or conservatives, believe that reason is too abstract a guide for the moral commitments of real human beings considered in the contexts of their actual life. Universalist reason denies that the diversity and particularity of individual human experience and the richness of possible relationships that define it for any individual person constitute not only our moral intuitions but also our very identities. This rationalist understanding of equality demands that such idiosyncratic elements not be counted in the moral identity of any individual person, because to do so would lead to differential treatment based on those elements. Someone else's significant impact on my own identity and moral intuitions should have no bearing on how I in turn respond to that person in terms of moral duty compared with others. Similarly, the different type or intensity of my relationships with others is morally irrelevant: equality means that all other persons have the same moral claim on me because they share with me the same unitary relationship with the universal rules of morality; thus, my moral obligation is universal across all persons with whom I come in contact. This obligation can be detailed in a relatively small set of universal rules.

Conversely, particularists are pluralists, seeing different value in the kinds of relations that typical people maintain and awarding therefore different degrees of moral obligation to the partners in relationships. Family members and friends legitimately command high moral obligation to their welfare, acquaintances less so, distant persons even less, and so on. This hierarchy of moral significance is grounded on the differential impact of those others on my own personal identity and sense of moral duty. For particularists, to deny this is first of all to deny the nature of human identity and relationships in a blind adherence to a seventeenth-century notion of both identity and human nature. Those relationships are diverse and their variety has differential impacts on the formation of human identity and one's moral sense.

Second, particularists insist that the abstractness of universalist morality has negative consequences in real-world situations that furthermore offend the moral sense of most real people. Both communitarians and feminists agree on this point, if on little else, because whether the examples are those given by MacIntyre regarding communal attachment or by Carole Gilligan regarding relationships based on care, the results of following moral rules instead of one's "habits of the heart" often lead to suffering on the part of those nearest to us.

Now, as this dispute relates to our general exploration of environmental human rights, two conclusions are possible from our adoption of the particularist position. First, we could jettison human rights altogether as a standard for morality as too abstract and universalist for the real world. Obviously I do not accept this approach, although other particularists do, including some feminists and most Marxists. Second, we could conclude that, from the standpoint of the communitarian position detailed in the previous chapters, it makes good (particularist) moral sense to acknowledge a preference for the environmental human rights of our own successor generation. Besides, and to be able to reject the first possible course, human rights are addressed to national communities anyway, so *legally* a particularist stance is already presumed within the present, real-world international regime of human rights.

These conclusions, although they fit well with the arguments of the previous chapters, do little to persuade universalists of my position, however. If it can be demonstrated that particularist methods or practices can lead to universalist goals, then the communitarian arguments for environmental human rights might have a better chance of widespread acceptance. The general appeal, even to universalists, of the particularist approach is that it acknowledges (or adds) multiple motives for individual persons to want to act morally – not only their reason but also their sentimental attachments lead them to selfless behavior on the part of *someone*, even if it usually is someone close to them. If somehow the strength of particularist ethics – the multiple and emotionally grounded sources of moral motivations – can be put into the service of the more abstracted universalist moral rationalism, the general effect might be to increase moral behavior overall.

Part of the argument for bringing together particularist and universalist moral ends follows in the next chapter, where I argue that a nationality basis for environmental human rights can lead to an overall increase in the global consensus on human rights as a foundation for morality. The rest of this chapter explores how the moral particularism of preferring the future generations of one's community (in the next section, of one's *nation*) can lead to an acceptable moral position for universalists. There are two arguments for how this can be accomplished, both of them anticipated by philosopher Robert Goodin. The first is his brief discussion about the pragmatism of dividing universal duties along local lines; the second is his more general argument for "protecting the vulnerable" as a general rule of universalist morality that nevertheless carries particularist moral commitments.

In his (1988) article-length discussion of Miller's defense of nationality as a moral category, Goodin (p. 678) proposes that we view the so-called special duties that particularists claim are due to those close to us rather as simply "general duties" due to every person but "distributed" to us for pragmatic reasons. Because we are closer to those persons, we can best deliver the necessary moral consideration; so, Goodin says, these general duties are presented to us as our "assigned responsibility." Significantly, those close to us do not have more or different moral claims on us, nor do we have special duties to them. Their claims and our correlated duties are of a *general* sort that all persons possess but that we are assigned owing to our proximity. On this accounting, therefore, all moral rules are impartial and universal, but the administration of them is particularist – distributing claims and assigning responsibility for acknowledging duties along, in this case, nationalistic lines.

Goodin's assigned responsibility approach succeeds somewhat in providing a sane and moderate resolution to portions of the universalist/particularist debate, but it does not resolve all of the problems. This is especially true in the issue we are exploring: the scope of moral obligation to future generations in response to environmental human rights. For example, it is somewhat difficult to see how the pragmatic and administrative division of duties relating to environmental rights along national lines could achieve one of its desired effects: improving the environment in the reciprocal way for both present and future generations necessary for calling it an obligation of justice, as explored in the last chapter. Because the natural environment is globally connected across artificial national borders, how is my recognition of my successor generations' environmental rights actually going to improve their environment, unless all (or at least adjacent) nations do the same? Furthermore, if my protection of successors' rights does not have the desired effect, then the reciprocal benefit to me does not necessarily follow either, thereby making this not an instance of justice across generations. What we need here is an actual universal moral principle that intrinsically operates in a particularist way, thereby rendering our adherence to it both particularist in practice and universalist in intent. Goodin's vulnerability principle fills that need.

In *Protecting the Vulnerable* (1985), Goodin presents an argument meant to bridge several divides within moral theory, including universalism/particularism, as well as the broader chasm separating consequentialist and deontological approaches. For Goodin, moral responsibility for the welfare of others is not grounded in either voluntary consent or the impartial application of moral rules, but rather in the existential fact that others are made vulnerable ("under threat of harm"; p. 110) both by our decisions and our actions. Therefore (p. 109), "we bear special responsibility for protecting those who are particularly vulnerable to us." The fact of their vulnerability alone commands our moral concern.

For Goodin, vulnerability determines moral responsibility toward a wider range of persons than most particularists acknowledge and in fact can account for responsibility even in most standard cases of responsibility usually invoked by universalists. The vulnerability of others, that is, can account for a very large portion of morality in general, including responsibility arising from promises, contracts, and business responsibilities, family relationships, friendships, and professional ethics – obligations also describable in terms of rights in a universalist system. Even more than Michael Ignatieff's (1984) argument for moral responsibility in response to the "needs of strangers," Goodin's principle of vulnerability invokes a powerful argument for acknowledging one's moral obligation across a broad range of one's life activities and experiences. He summarizes (p. 11):

> What is crucial in my view is that others are depending on us. They are particularly vulnerable to our actions and choices. That, I argue, is the true source of all the standard special responsibilities that we so readily acknowledge. The same considerations of vulnerability that make our obligations to our families, friends, clients, and compatriots especially strong can also give rise to similar responsibilities toward a much larger group of people who stand in none of the standard special relationships to us.

The principle of vulnerability as a central part of a theory of morality is especially well suited for the interconnected world of the twenty-first century. As I have discussed elsewhere (Hiskes, 1998), the idea of moral responsibility has been greatly affected by the development of new knowledge and new technologies in a variety of fields, all of which bring the impacts (or the awareness of them) of any person's decisions or actions into the everyday lives of a wide range of other people. That is to say, my decisions about energy consumption, transportation, sexual activity, personal hygiene, smoking, and even leisure activities reverberate in other people's lives, enmeshing all of us in a web of risk and responsibility in which we are all vulnerable to each other for the collective impact of our private decisions. Because we are, as Goodin says, mutually "under threat of harm" from each other, we have moral responsibility to respond to the vulnerability that seems to radiate from us all.[3]

The principle of vulnerability offers a morality for an interconnected world. As such it has an apparent appeal for environmentalism generally, because as stated before, any environmental or ecological theory presumes the interconnection of all natural life. Goodin, in fact, concludes (pp. 179–186) that environmental protection is a moral obligation under the principle, because nature's vulnerability to human depredations is beyond dispute. Here, Goodin acknowledges, vulnerability is being construed somewhat more broadly, because what is being affected are environmental "states" rather than any particular person's specific interests. Because in the long (sometimes short) run all humans' interests are negatively impacted by deterioration of the environment, we are under moral obligation not to increase human vulnerability through our interventions in the natural world.

It is here that the real value of Goodin's approach for environmental human rights makes its presence known, although not primarily because Goodin derives an environmental protection argument from the principle of vulnerability. The real reasons have to do with how future generations are vulnerable to us and with how obligations to (future) others are distributed according to their level of vulnerability to our actions or decisions.

Goodin does not anticipate my argument in Chapter 3 for intergenerational justice based on reflexive reciprocity because he postulates that (p. 177), "no analysis of intergenerational justice that is cast even vaguely in terms of reciprocity can hope to succeed." Nevertheless, he argues that present generations have a clear moral obligation to their successors owing to the present's "unilateral power over the generations that succeed us" (p. 177). Future generations clearly depend on policy or personal decisions that we make today in terms of resource allocation and depletion, waste disposal, and in many other areas that add up to a conclusion that "the only way they will have anything at all is for us to leave it to them" (p. 177). Therefore, they are obviously "vulnerable" to the

---

3 Goodin recognizes that when stated as such, the principle of vulnerability is essentially a consequentialist form of ethics; however, his discussion of why it is a consequentialism that even nonconsequentialists could embrace is enlightening and persuasive, if not particularly important for my purposes here. See pp. 114–117 for his exploration of the place of vulnerability in nonconsequentialist moral theory.

choices we make, and we in turn must be cognizant of our moral obligations to them as we make decisions affecting the future.

Furthermore, we have special moral obligations to the future generations of our own community. Just as particularists argue that special obligations are owed to those closest to us emotionally, Goodin insists (p. 121) that those closest physically or temporally are also due special concern. They deserve this particularist preference not because of his first pragmatic, distributional argument, but because they are especially vulnerable:

> On balance, persons relatively near to us in space and time probably *will* be rather more vulnerable to us. Their interests are more likely to be affected more heavily by our own actions and choices than are the interests of persons more distant; and our nearer neighbors in space and time are more likely to be depending upon us, more or less exclusively, for assistance and protection.... My analysis would seem to show *some* bias toward our own "kind," however defined. Still that bias must not be absolute. (emphases Goodin's)

There lies our argument for giving moral preference to the future generations of "people like us," our own successors. This is an argument from moral particularism, but because it is grounded in the moral bindingness of vulnerability, this argument also, as Goodin notes, is not absolute and therefore appeals to universalists. That is important for its applicability as an argument from human rights, which is, as we have seen, a distinctly universalist moral position. We therefore have arrived at a convincing argument for recognizing our moral obligation to respect the environmental human rights of future generations, an argument that spans both particularist and universalist perspectives. Furthermore, it is an argument that validates our intuition that we owe special moral consideration to the future generations of our own community. What remains, however, is to ask whether it is valid to describe that community in terms of nationality: is our obligation to respect the environmental human rights of future generations legitimately restricted to the successors of our own nation?

NATIONALITY AND THE OBLIGATION TO THE RIGHTS OF THE FUTURE

Up to this point in my argument I have been using the term "community" in a somewhat loose or nontechnical manner, thereby avoiding excess specificity in deciding who exactly is the addressee of environmental human rights. In a legal sense, of course, the relevant community for any human right is the nation state, because states and their governments are the addressees of human rights in the international community, as delineated by international covenants like the UDHR. Besides, from a policy perspective, the effectiveness of environmental human rights depends either on laws passed by national governments or international treaties signed by those governments that seek to protect the rights of present and future citizens.

Nevertheless, because we now have an argument for why from a moral point of view it is legitimate to protect preferentially the environmental human rights of our own future generations, it is clear that we now must be specific about who "we" actually are. What is the extent of our community, whose members and future generations are our concern? Who are the "people like us," for whom the protection of their rights reciprocally functions as a protection of our own? Are our community's borders the same as the political borders demarking our nation's territorial limits, and if they are, does nature's ignorance of them matter in our legal, political, and policy considerations concerning environmental human rights?

This last question goes far in explaining why immigration issues have come to dominate the political discourse of some Western nations, certainly including the United States. The questions also have moved to center stage in political theory and philosophy circles with the publication of Rawls's *The Law of Peoples* (1999). Rawls distinguishes five sorts of societies, or "peoples," and does so employing explicitly political criteria. In doing so, he lays the groundwork for recognizing which communities or "peoples" are moral in the sense of being capable of protecting human rights and furthering justice, and which are not. The first two categories of "liberal" and "decent" peoples have the right and obligation to further the interests of their own successors. The latter three (i.e., outlaw states, burdened societies, benevolent absolutisms) do not, because doing so will perpetuate their unjust societies. It is in the criteria for what constitutes a people (especially a "liberal" one) and distinguishes it from a nation/state that Rawls makes distinctions of use in our evaluation of "nationality" as an acceptable determinant of obligation to protect others' rights.

For Rawls, a liberal people has three basic features: "a reasonably just constitutional democratic government that serves their fundamental interests; citizens united by what are called 'common sympathies'; and finally, a moral nature" (p. 23). The first feature is what makes it clear that by "people" Rawls is referring explicitly to a political society, part of the "society of peoples" by which he refers to the community of international law. By distinguishing between different governmental systems in his characterizations of peoples, Rawls makes it clear that his focus is on extant nation states. The second two features, however, are essential in what I have been calling a community, and, I would argue, for what are usually termed "nations" in a more inclusive understanding of the term that is not limited to nation states. This broadening of the idea of peoples as nations beyond merely the modern nation state is necessary for our understanding of the obligation of nations to protect the environmental human rights of their future generations.

Skipping ahead first to Rawls's third feature of a liberal people – a moral nature – it is relatively uncontroversial given his other commitments and needs only a word or two here. Liberal peoples are "both reasonable and rational, and their rational conduct . . . is similarly constrained by their sense of what is reasonable" (p. 25). Furthermore, liberal people express their reasonableness through the offer of "fair terms of cooperation to other people" (p. 25). This picture of liberal morality we explored fully in Chapter 2 in our discussion of Rawls's view of tit-for-tat reciprocity, and therefore its obvious limitations need not be addressed again. Suffice it to say that Rawls again is treating morality here in an expressly political way – as the product of voluntary consent by means of the original position – but we will deem it acceptable given his purpose of differentiating between different public moralities as parts of different peoples or political societies.

It is in his second feature of shared "common sympathies" that Rawls introduces a notion of nationality of interest to moral particularists and also therefore to my argument for preferential treatment of one's own successors' human rights. Rawls cites (p. 23; n. 17) J. S. Mill's well-known definition of nationality to support the common sympathies requirement of peoplehood:

> A portion of mankind may be said to constitute a Nationality, if they are united among themselves by common sympathies, which do not exist between them and any others – which make them cooperate with each other more willingly than with other people, desire to be under the same government, and desire that it should be government by themselves, or a portion of themselves, exclusively.

Mill's notion of nationality is grounded on two specific elements included to some extent by Rawls in his idea of a "people," but that I want to separate out of Rawls's broader, more political definition to use as my focus for nationality as a basis for moral preference. They are, first, a shared concept of identity; second, a belief in shared citizenship that carries special obligations to fellow citizens.

All current discussions of the meaning of community, as we have seen in previous chapters, stress the appreciation of a shared communal identity. That identity is both amorphous and specific, enough so of each that members easily recognize each other in a general, unspoken way as fellow members yet remain open to new members by the embracing of specific characteristics, beliefs, relationships, and so forth that are available for adoption by those willing to join. There is no necessary connection between the feelings of communal belonging or membership on the one hand and nationality on the other, yet it is indisputable that, for good or ill, most persons recognize their membership in the nation as a primary form of communal attachment. It is an issue of some moment among philosophers and others whether this association of nationality with community is a positive or negative feature of modern politics and society. I want to argue, relying on several current theorists of nationality, that Mill's understanding of national identity as grounded in both shared sympathies and practices of citizenship elevates the relationship of fellow nationals to the moral one of communal connection. In this effort I shall also invoke some of Hannah Arendt's arguments concerning the meaning of human liberty and citizenship in the face of late modernity's unique threat of totalitarianism. It is that threat, more recently regenerated under the guise of "globalization," that brings to nationality and citizenship a criticality in the preservation of human identity, liberty, and morality.

The whole concept of nationality has about it today the musty scent of an old coat no longer fit for public appearance. I think there are two reasons for this, one historical and one pressingly current. The first comes down from the struggles against repressive nations in the latter half of the twentieth century. First Nazi Germany and Mussolini's Italy, and then Stalin's Russia represent for many today the dangerous consequence of a too-fervent belief in nation and nationality. Since the end of the Cold War a long list of other candidates is easily recognized: Cuba, China, Serbia, Iraq, Iran, and many more. Arendt's magisterial treatment of the new phenomenon of totalitarianism first in *Eichmann in Jerusalem* (1965) and later in *The Origins of Totalitarianism* (1979) presented this newest form of the nation state as a unique and terrifying new threat to human flourishing in every sense. Not only morality, but human liberty, sociality, and even identity seemed set to disappear in the new form of nationhood. Arendt, of course, provided a political solution to totalitarianism that remains vigorously circumscribed within the nation state, requiring as it does an active citizenship alive to the requirements of political choice and public morality. We shall explore Arendt's vision of a healthy politics in a moment, and doing so will make it clear that although modern nationalism can lead to totalitarian oppression, this is not an inevitable consequence. Nationalism today manifests both healthy and unhealthy forms; only the former is truly communitarian.

The second reason for the denigration of nationality as a moral concept has to do with current emphases on globalization and its attendant technologies that seem to render national borders a quaint irrelevancy. In a sense, of course, human rights are both part and product of this approach. Although most lists of human rights include what have historically been known as citizenship (in the nation state) rights, the very change in the adjective from "natural" or "inalienable" to "human" seems to signal a change of focus away from past political categories. To continue to think of human rights in the context of nation states somehow makes them more contingent on the particularities of individual nations than their status as "human" would seem to allow. The success of human rights seems in important ways then to require the evolution of the species away from the political categories of modernity and toward a new "global" reality. This focus is largely that of the next chapter.

The first type of case against the idea of nationality as a moral category comes from arguments presented by John O'Neill (1994). O'Neill insists that states cannot be seen as moral communities because they are not by nature communal in the sense in which communitarians mean the term – as creating what Charles Taylor (1989) called the "encumbered self." The level of reciprocity, interdependence, and shared meaning that communitarians like Taylor, MacIntyre, and Sandel ascribe to moral communities is precisely what is lacking in the modern nation state, according to O'Neill. This lack is particularly evident in a state housing one of Rawls's liberal peoples, O'Neill continues, because such a nation "is one of the main vehicles for the construction of the unencumbered self and the disappearance of ties of community. Hence the association of communitarianism with the defence of the nation is also a mistake" (p. 136).

The modern nation state, beginning in the sixteenth century, O'Neill asserts, was founded on the disintegration of the social ties that communitarians identify as those of community. This loosening of ties was exacerbated by the association of politics with capitalist free markets within the liberal state, and specifically with the delineation of the rights and powers necessary for individual persons to succeed in the economic realm. As the liberal state came to mean primarily the protection of the liberal individual person's rights and powers to compete, any hope of maintaining community at the national level quickly eroded. The power to protect individual rights became the chief defining characteristic of the modern nation, and concentrating that power into the hands of government fundamentally altered the nature of human association. As compared with loyalties to others based on communal attachment, loyalty to the nation state became grounded solely on the fact the state's power to protect.

This concentration of political power, like that of the rights of property, changes the nature of an individual's ties and loyalties to others. In claiming a monopoly of legitimate power the modern state demands of its citizens a loyalty that overrides all others.... No loyalty to another authority or community that might conflict with that of the state can be recognized. The modern nation state which inherits the appropriated powers of the prince likewise demands an overriding loyalty that corresponds to its claims to a monopoly of power. (p. 137)

Given the monopoly of power and loyalty characterizing the state in O'Neill's eyes, to also grant it the romantic associations of moral community is to run headlong into the Arendtian nightmare of totalitarianism.

O'Neill notes (p. 138) that the communitarian understanding of nationality begins with the conservatism of nineteenth-century thinkers Herder and Schiller – a development much later than that of the modern state itself. Furthermore, these German theorists and subsequent communitarian thinkers like Taylor and MacIntyre present a distinctively affective, nonrational understanding of the state as community. It is this view of nationalism, in Daniel Weinstock's (1996, p. 87) words, as "essentially an affective phenomenon, the manifestation of emotion and unreason, of atavistic drives rather than of rational deliberation," that frightens liberal critics of both nationalism and community. In their view, such affective ties are not only ancillary to the modern state but also dangerous in their conflation of nationality with community.

O'Neill's challenge to defenders of nationality is a serious one, because it confronts the often illiberal nature of modern communitarianism. As evidenced in Chapter 2, however, not all communitarians trace their roots back to nineteenth-century conservatism, and not all believers in the communal potential of nationality need do so either. Nationality theorists David Miller, Margaret Moore, and Yael Tamir envision liberal national communities that can provide the communal ties that both elevate concern for one's compatriots to the level of moral obligation without at the same time moving the community toward totalitarian commitment. The key to achieving both is to wed communal identity with democratic politics.

THE DEMOCRATIC RETRIEVAL OF COMMUNAL NATIONALISM

Miller (1997) begins by noting that the liberal fear of nationality and community tends to "overstate the role played by sentiment in forming national communities" (p. 74).

It is true that shared symbols and history can give rise to the kind of blind (sometimes dangerous) national loyalty based more on romantic ideals or emotional ties, but not all nations emulate "Red Sox Nation" but are grounded instead on shared self-interest and the common good as well as a strong recognition of mutual obligation. Tamir stresses (1993, 99ff) that nationality refers mostly to shared identity, an identity from which "deep and important obligations flow." These obligations are not merely derived from sentiment or "fellow feeling" but are grounded on a Kantian rationality that makes justice an obligation not only toward countrymen but also toward all human beings. It is not new that community is constitutive of identity, of course, but for Tamir it is crucial to see that nationality delivers that very constitutive effect on an individual person's senses of self and of justice and is therefore communal in nature at the same time that it enhances the idea of justice.[4]

Moore (2001) and Miller (1988, 1995, 1997) bring an expressly political cast to national identity, expanding beyond its affective and morally obligating features stressed by Tamir. Moore recognizes that an essential part of nationhood is not just shared subjective identity but pursuit of common goals, usually referred to as the common good, through accepted and shared institutions governing distributions of power, resources, and reward. This good can be interpreted, as it is by Hurka (1997), as referring only to objective goods, that is, goods not partial only to one's own nation. Hurka is concerned to ensure that legitimating nationalism on the grounds that it produces a common good and therefore presumes shared notions of goodness, and discriminates between some common goods that are objectively "good," such as human rights, and "bad" nationalist goods, that would underpin, for example, a shared Nazi national culture. For Hurka, nationalism can be either a good or bad thing, depending on the objective value of the good pursued by any particular nation. As he states (p. 151), "[i]f national attachment rests partly on the belief that one's culture is good, it is important that that belief is true, which requires the culture to be, in fact, good."

Miller's approach is somewhat different from Hurka's, as Moore points out (p. 35), and more recognizably liberal for its focus on process rather than outcome. For Miller, what matters in legitimating nationalism is not necessarily the good produced, but the political institutions employed in the pursuit. It is here that Moore agrees with Miller that what matters in assessing the virtue of nationalism in any particular case – and including the assessment of obligations that arise, as Tamir argues, from national identity – are the politics that define a national public culture. Moore insists (p. 37) that it is

---

[4] For a contrary view to Tamir's argument that national commitments make justice possible, see Authur Ripstein (1997), "Context, Continuity, and Fairness," in Robert McKim and Jeff McMahan, eds., **The Morality of Nationalism**. New York: Oxford.

crucial to view nations as "politically embodied"; it is from that view alone that derives "the force of the argument that we have (nonrenounceable) obligations to the nation." Such obligations pertain only if the "practices and institutions" within national politics are themselves worthy of obligation. For Miller, those politics must be democratic, manifesting the features of what Rawls calls a "decent people." What makes the people "decent" are its commitments to democratic principles and institutions; what makes the people a nation is its citizens' active engagement in democratic politics. It is this combination of democratic institutions and participatory citizens that finally makes a nation a community – a liberal *and* moral one that need not fear slipping into totalitarianism.

Miller (1995, 21–27) lists five attributes of a nation that make it clear that he is speaking of liberal and democratic form of national community. First, a nation is grounded in belief or, as Mill would have it, in "shared sympathies" or a subjective awareness of "one another as compatriots," that share "characteristics of a relevant kind" (p. 22). Second, a nation is rooted in time, embodying an "identity that embodies historical continuity," that embraces both a past and anticipated future (p. 23). Third, national identities are "active" not passive; they constitute and reaffirm themselves constantly as "communities that do things together, take decisions, achieve results, and so on" (p. 24). Fourth, nations occupy a physical locale, connecting "a group of people to a geographical place" (p. 24). Finally, "a national identity requires that the people who share it should have something in common, a set of characteristics that. . . . I prefer to describe as a common public culture" (p. 25). It is the third and fifth characteristics that mark Miller's view of nationality as distinctly democratic and communal, and therefore both deserving of moral obligation and capable of moral attachment.

A nation becomes recognizably a community when its citizens act together politically, making decisions within a shared history and set of beliefs that mark them as an organic "body politic." Democratic participation is crucial in the process of community building and maintaining, for it is as active citizens that members acknowledge the "shared sympathies" that bind them together in a public culture with a future as well as a past. Without democratic institutions and practices, nations still exist as political entities, but not as moral communities because there is no guarantee that public space exists for citizens to engage in the moral discourse and decision making that community requires. The nation as a whole will generate moral rules, but the rules will not be the result of a free and open moral discourse. There might well be moral authority in the nondemocratic state; there will not be moral community.

The liberty guaranteed by democratic institutions is a prerequisite for citizens publicly to share their beliefs, their ideas, and their histories in creating and sustaining a communal identity. It is as citizens of a democratic nation that we recognize special moral obligations to each other that take precedence over those that we owe to others. Because it sustains that moral engagement, it is "the intrinsic value of citizenship," Andrew Mason (1997) concludes, that offers "the most promising account" of why we have special moral obligations to compatriots.

What characterizes citizenship must be the rights necessary to participate in the determination of those obligations and in the free assumption of them. Without those rights what exists is a community of force, not a moral community. Those rights are the human rights of democracy. Richard Dagger (1985) concludes that "we should grant priority to our compatriots because, *ceteris paribus*, we owe it to them. Why? Because there is a special relationship, entailing special rights and obligations, between those who share citizenship in a political community" (p. 443). That relationship, Dagger claims, is defined by reciprocity, the very relation we determined in Chapter 2 to be at the heart of moral community. Those rights entailed by the reciprocal relationship of citizens are what we name human rights today, and it is the reciprocity of citizenship for Dagger that leads citizens mutually to protect their human rights. "Compatriots take priority," Dagger stipulates, "because we owe it to them as a matter of reciprocity. Everyone, compatriot or not, has a claim to our respect and concern... but those who join with us in cooperative enterprises have a claim to special recognition" (p. 446).

The convergence of nationality with moral community requires then that the nation be a democratic one, and it must be, because of the protection for human rights that democracies provide. This is why it is only with great difficulty that it is possible to conceive of human rights apart from democracy. The argument for decoupling human rights from democracy can be made,[5] but not without restricting the number of rights to a precious few. What makes such theories of human rights so "thin" is the loss of the variety and large number of rights necessary for the creation of moral communities by free citizens engaged in the moral discourse and decision making of politics. Only nations that are democratic enough to be moral communities – not merely moral authorities – can protect the environmental rights of their citizens, present and future. Those nations, those communities, are intrinsically democratic,

---

[5] See for instance, Lin Chun (2001), "Human Rights and Democracy: The Case for Decoupling." **International Journal of Human Rights** 5: 19–44. Chun relies on an extremely "thin" theory of rights, recognizing the right to life "sustained by material subsistence and physical security" as the only real human right.

and because they are their citizens are free to take on themselves the moral obligation to ensure a green future.

CONCLUSION: THE *VITA ACTIVA* OF DEMOCRACY AND THE ENVIRONMENTAL PROMISE OF NATIONALISM

Hannah Arendt began her journey across the mind and soul of late twentieth-century politics by examining the plight of "stateless citizens" – subjects of the modern state best represented by Jews during and after the Holocaust. These modern "pariahs," as Arendt refers to them, have little role as citizens and even less as members of a political community. They are part of the "social" but not the "political": they can become "parvenus," marginally acceptable socially by virtue of having money but never truly received as citizens. They lack the history and the shared public character of citizens who build together their own political and therefore social environment. These pariahs and parvenus of the modern state anticipate the development of totalitarianism through their victimhood – they are the victims of historical forces rather than citizens who through their political life together shape their own destiny as autonomous moral agents, a capacity, Hannah Fenichel Pitkin (1998) notes, "exclusively of human beings."

For Arendt, the task of modern politics, if it is to avoid totalitarianism, is to release citizens into the "vita activa," the political life of free moral agents engaged together as "builders of worlds or cobuilders of a common world" (2003, 139). It is this life of political action that brings human dignity, and it is captured only in the realm of the modern nation that embraces democratic discourse and deliberation as the means to a common life. It is only such a community that can withstand the totalitarian threat, because it delivers the connection and meaningfulness of shared participation in a common world without the loss of self that drives the totalitarian "mass society." The citizen who holds rights of political participation – the "juridical person" – is the first casualty on the "road to total domination" (2003, 128). Protecting those human rights and keeping them ever fresh through participation in the moral community of the modern nation is what keeps totalitarianism at bay.

In short, democratic politics turn nations into communities and deliver the citizens into a shared realm of meaning within which freedom is possible. That realm for Arendt – and still today for human rights advocates – is defined by nationality. The choice between a conscious and active democratic politics or the dictatorial effects of an inert citizenry determines nationality's impact. Democratic politics as the active life of citizens engaged in joint decision making gives to nationality its moral and communal status; the inactivity of "mass society" makes nations lifeless politically and turns community into tyranny.[6]

As community members of democratic nations then, citizens have the obligation to consider the welfare of their successor citizens. Their successors are already members of the community as defined by its own political institutions that, like all decision-making bodies, anticipate the future. As we will see in Chapter 6, this applies especially to constitutions among all political institutions that require this forward-looking inclusiveness regarding future citizens; therefore constitutionalism itself contains a special reverence for the rights of successor generations, including their rights to a healthy environment. Rather than showing particularist prejudice or contributing to injustice, this moral partiality in favor of one's own successor compatriots is the only way democratically to include them in the "vita activa" of community life. By adopting democratic means, the community has become a nation, and at the same time made democratic protections of future citizens a top priority.

Of course, not all nations today are democratic moral communities, so how can they all come to respect the environmental rights of their future generations? Partly this is a question of the universality of human rights, and partly a matter of consensus among nations. Given the global nature of the physical environment, however, such universal respect for future generations and their environmental rights is a prerequisite to any real or lasting improvement in our jointly shared physical world. Across national borders today there is less than unanimous agreement on either the universality of human rights or on the possibility of consensus on which human rights deserve protection. Every culture, whether organized democratically or not, contains within it a palpable and vibrant sense of its own future and the needs of its own descendants who will populate it. Whether this sense within *each* nation is enough to bring *all* nations together into a global consensus on the universality of environmental human rights is the issue to which we now turn.

---

[6] Pitkin (1998) succinctly characterizes the difference between political and social connection in Arendt's view. Pitkin comments, "the social is a particular mode of interrelationship among people, a form of togetherness in which each thinks himself an isolated atom and behaves accordingly, but they in fact generate collective results that include the continual enforcement of such thinking and behavior on each other, and thus their 'normalization' into homogeneity. That is why Arendt speaks of them both as isolated atoms and also as congealed together too tightly, into a mass. For Arendt, this social way of living together stands in sharpest contrast to the political way, in which autonomous and responsible individual persons, recognizing their objective interdependence, jointly take such charge of it as human beings can – which of course is never perfect, complete, or lasting. This social kind of 'unitedness of many into one is basically antipolitical; it is the very opposite of the togetherness' characterizing political membership" (p. 194).

5

Toward a Global Consensus on Environmental Human Rights

Think not forever of yourselves, O Chiefs, nor of your own generation. Think of continuing generations of our families, think of our grandchildren and of those yet unborn, whose faces are coming from beneath the ground.

Peacemaker, Founder of the Iroquois Confederacy

Our consideration in the last chapter of nationalism within a globalized world of human rights and environmental obligations reveals a paradox within current human rights thinking and application. Human rights theory and practice today manifest both an increasing global consensus on human rights as a category of legitimacy, while at the same time expressing a "third-generation" insistence on honoring the diversity of individual cultures and their right to maintain their historic norms. On the one hand, Jack Donnelly (2007, 282) insists that human rights "have become ideologically hegemonic in international society. Not only do few states today directly challenge international human rights, a surprisingly small number even seriously contend that large portions of the Universal Declaration [of Human Rights] do not apply to them." Conversely, James N. Rosenau (2002, 153) notes what he calls the "fragmentation" of human rights as they are "localized" into the many specific cultures once devoid of any sensitivity to the idea of rights. As Michael Ignatieff (1999) concludes, "human rights has gone global, but it has also gone local."

In terms of the argument for environmental human rights and intergenerational justice that I have presented thus far, this paradox of globalism and parochialism has an interesting manifestation. My argument asks whether it is possible to enhance the chances of a global consensus on the moral imperative of human rights (including environmental rights) by arguing for the environmental rights of only my own society's successor generations. This is tantamount to looking for a global effect from a local commitment. I argue that it is possible to foster a universal concern both for the global environment

and for all people's environmental rights (including those of future generations) that is grounded in the parochial communal attachments of individual
persons to their own culture and society. The last chapter explored whether
those local attachments can produce a global moral commitment to protecting
global environmental rights.

The irony level of the argument thus far is heightened when we are careful to keep our overall object in view: the global environment. A focus on
the communal or parochial protection of environmental human rights as the
foundation for a global consensus is doubly paradoxical because the environment itself is difficult to construe in any but global terms. It therefore seems
uniquely difficult to parse individual or societal moral obligations arising from
environmental rights to achieve the global effect of a healthier environment
for ourselves and those who come after. For example, how could there be a
global agreement about my own or my own society's obligations to the environmental human rights of others, especially if those obligations vary in different
societies?

In fact, this is the very issue that caused the United States, justifiably or not, to
withdraw from the Kyoto Protocol agreement on protecting the environment.
The Bush administration argued that it was unfair to levy differential levels of
environmental obligation on different countries, singling out specifically the
United States, China, and India, the latter two being designated "developing
countries" and therefore given more latitude and time in meeting environmental goals. When environmental human rights are considered, then, global
solutions that rely on local efforts seem fraught with political and moral arguments leading away from, not toward, a global consensus. If this turns out to be
true, then my argument is not just paradoxical or ironic; it is simply wrong –
neither intergenerational environmental justice nor environmental human
rights can be secured by focusing on how individual communities internalize
these goals.

In this chapter, I shall argue that in fact we should view the possibility of
institutionalizing environmental human rights on a societal level as the first
step in the continuing efforts to achieve intergenerational environmental justice globally, and toward reaching a more complete international consensus
on human rights of all kinds. In the next section, that argument begins with
an exploration of what globalization has meant and continues to mean for the
institutionalization of human rights within and between societies. Others have
written on this topic as well, and I shall rely on some of those writings to develop a special environmental variant of a "global human rights consensus."

As a metaphor for such a global environmental consensus grounded on
national cultural norms, in the subsequent section I shall explore how a

concern for later generations' environmental rights resembles concerns for rights violations as evidenced in national apologies for past abuses. The similarities between the two areas of human rights practice are interestingly related in terms of how both time and cultural specificity help to arrive at global agreement. Although apologies naturally refer to past abuses, environmental human rights employ some of the same conceptualizations and the language of obligation in a different but related "pay it forward" attribution of responsibility for future environmental consequences.

Finally, respecting the environmental human rights of successor generations is directly analogous to respecting the rights of self-determination for individual states as a principle on which there is considerable global consensus. In significant ways, environmental human rights are a foundational form of self-determination rights, because controlling environmental effects of all kinds is essentially what self-determination (or identity creation) means in a world populated by others and their effects on our collective "selves." We saw in Chapter 2 how modern self-identity is always socially constructed by those who share our environment. In the final section of this chapter we shall explore how cultural identity can include a global construction of environmental human rights.

By comparing a global consensus on environmental human rights to those developing around the issues of national apologies and self-determination, we can also prepare for the discussion in Chapter 6 concerning the legal status of environmental human rights. Putting into practice intergenerational environmental justice based on rights requires some legal precedents that can be viewed both logically and legally as relevant in a constitutional sense. The areas of human rights law concerning apologies and self-determination might supply the needed legal concepts and agreement to undergird those precedents.

GLOBALIZATION AND HUMAN RIGHTS

When embarking on our present topic, Upenda Baxi (2002, 170) admonishes that the "'globalization' of human rights is a process in search of a careful description." Such care is particularly required, Baxi continues, because the process of human rights globalization "suppresses, even supplants, when expedient, the rhetoric of universality of human rights" (p. 171). One might easily assume just the opposite – that when it comes to human rights, globalization and universalization would be coterminous events or processes. Baxi and others make it clear that the two are not identical or even necessarily mutually supporting, however. Human rights institutions, law, and politics might indeed attain a global reach, yet that does not mean that human rights will have achieved a universally accepted definition.

Furthermore, it could equally well be argued that globalization as a separate phenomenon threatens human rights in general, whether they are perceived as universal or not. As Michael Goodhart ironically notes (2003, 936), "[S]trangely, while there is no consensus among scholars that there are any such things as universal human rights, there is nonetheless widespread agreement that globalization poses a universal threat to human rights." This perception of the globalized threat to human rights – especially to economic human rights – is, as Goodhart notes, widely shared among scholars as well as practitioners. Not all agree, however; one prominent human rights scholar, Harold Koh, is so comfortable discussing what in his view is the tranquil, mutually self-supporting partnership of globalization and human rights that he refers to universal human rights as the "third globalization – the rise of transnational human rights networks of both public and private actors" (quoted in Steiner and Alston, 2000, p. 1310). Clearly, exploring the relationship between globalization as a phenomenon and the global institutionalization of human rights is an essential first step in considering whether a universal consensus on human rights of any kind is achievable.

So what is globalization, and what are its effects on human rights? Both questions press on human rights theorists and activists today, but there remains little consensus on either. The discussion tends to diverge according to whether the effects concern political, cultural, or economic human rights, and different levels of agreement among scholars emerge on each topic. What I shall suggest is that despite such persistent disagreement, consensus is possible on both the meaning of environmental human rights and on measuring globalization's impact on them. Such a consensus on environmental human rights can pave the way globally for further agreement on which others are truly universal human rights.

Defining Globalization

Definitions of globalization abound, and considering them brings certainty only to the realization that it remains a contested term, one that, for David Held and Anthony McGrew (2007), might even refer to a phenomenon in decline. For many, globalization refers mostly to the economic aspects of market integration and invokes (often negative) images of the role of international financial institutions initially created at the Bretton Woods conference in 1944. For instance, in calling globalization the "second great transformation," Rhoda Howard-Hassmann memorably defines the phenomenon as "the final assault of capitalism on all those areas of the globe that previously escaped it" (2005, 5). The historic capitalist institutions leading this transforming global assault include the International Monetary Fund (IMF) and World Bank, followed in 1948 by the General Agreement on Tariffs and Trade (GATT), and extended by the North American Free Trade Agreement (NAFTA) in 1991. Viewed through the role of these institutions, globalization often refers primarily to world economic processes, or indeed is taken to be a synonym for global capitalism (Korten, 1995). For G. John Ikenberry (2007, 42) it was the United States that "launched the world on the path of market globalization"; therefore, if globalization is a synonym for global capitalism, it is equally one for "American hegemony."

Others see globalization as less threatening and as a more varied and amorphous process resulting, in Mary Robinson's words (2003), "in a world of more connections – markets, people, ideas linked as never before." Similarly, Micheline Ishay (2004, 256) offers that globalization is best seen as "an amalgamation of a host of international processes," the dimensions of which have "undergone substantial change since the beginning of the cold war, change that has had different impacts across countries, groups, and classes." Robert Keohane and Joseph Nye (2000, 110–111) suggest that "globalization is best seen as a set of linked yet distinct dimensions: economic, military, cultural, social, and environmental." Finally, Alison Brysk (2002, 6) summarizes that "globalization is an ensemble of developments that make the world a single place, changing the meaning and importance of distance and national identity in world affairs."

Although the global connections invoked by these scholars are often linked to large-scale institutions like financial or political ones such as the World Trade Organization (WTO), Richard Falk (2002) rightly points out that not all globalization is "from above," an overlay by powerful organizations seeking expansive economic movement. Indeed, much of the impetus of globalization can be seen as emanating from resistance to just such organizations on the part of local groups organized around mostly national issues but often linked through Internet contact. Falk refers to the "protesters in the streets and their governmental allies" as constituting the other side of the globalizing process: "globalization from below" (2002, 61).

Falk's characterization of the two sides of globalization expands the term to include global cultural developments like the adoption of human rights as the universalized argot within a world of protest. Even if Howard-Hassmann (2004, 6) is justified in referring to the global language of human rights as "part of the general cultural emanation from the West," that language is transmitted globally through a vast network of global media, delivering images of resistance in the name of human rights. Obviously, human rights constitute more than a language of resistance, but Falk is correct that their widespread invocation is itself a persistent feature of a new global political reality, a reality that underwrites Koh's optimism concerning his "third globalization."

Significantly, the whole regime of human rights presumes a globalized consensus on their justification and efficacy, even as they are invoked as antidotes to globalization itself. Even without universal agreement on their content, human rights posit a globalized and globalizing culture that pervades both international institutions of finance and governance as well as local movements defending either the victims of globalization or the cultures threatened by it.

As frequently opposing claims, human rights and globalization represent, for Monshipouri and his colleagues (2003, x) what they term "competing universalisms, [suggesting] two interlocking ideas. First, globalization and human rights both claim to be universal ideas, but at many levels they place conflicting demands on actors. Second, each of these universalizing processes evokes resistance, but resistance in the modern world is seldom willing to present itself as localistic or particularistic, and may stake a claim to universalist pretensions of its own."

Falk's "resistance from below" usually manifests itself locally, but Monshipouri et al. are correct that what are being claimed in local protests are not local preferences or nationally specific interests but *universal claims of a localistic nature*. In the face of globalizing tendencies arise local movements or attempts to reassert – on human rights grounds – the universal importance of the local: the connections that tie individual people to particular places, ideas, traditions, and beliefs. As Carol Gould (2004, 118) characterizes these contrasting movements, "increasing globalization and universalization of culture worldwide have paradoxically been matched by increasing cultural pluralism and separatism. These two conflicting trends are reflected in cosmopolitanism or the homogenization of cultures, on the one hand, and in claims to cultural autonomy or to ethnic and nationalist chauvinisms, on the other."

Reclaiming or protecting the local therefore is also part of globalization, as paradoxical as that sounds, and those claims are made in the universalist language of human rights, albeit a new generation of rights usually known as group or culture rights. If globalization is the story of postmodernity, Terry Eagleton asserts (1999, 264), only one half of that story has to do with institutional, economic, or governmental integration. "The other, more positive half is a much more radical retrieval of the local, the vernacular, the somatic, the communitarian, the unincorporable particular history, in the teeth of an apparently homogenized globe." Part of globalization, in other words, is a widespread and growing resistance to the loss of the local and its connections, traditions, and values. As ironic as it sounds, "we may best consider contemporary globalization in its most general sense as a form of institutionalization of the two-fold process involving the universalization of particularism and the particularization of universalism" (Robertson and Inglis, 1992, 2).

This dialectic of global and local has also reconfigured the institutional landscape characterizing human rights in the age of globalization. As Margaret Keck and Kathryn Sikkink's important contribution (1998) makes clear, singular new elements both in international politics and the politics of human rights are networks of activists united by new communications technologies and activated by a shared mission of making global human rights aims achievable in local terms and settings. These "transnational advocacy networks" are unique to our global age – they are what populate Koh's third globalization – and they bridge the local and global as "networks of activists, distinguishable largely by the centrality of principled ideas or values in motivating their formation" (Keck and Sikkink, 1998, 2). These are "activists beyond borders," relying on new information technology to bring global human rights principles to local political conflicts.

Because globalization operates within (or stimulates) this global/local dialectic, local attachments or beliefs strive for universal validity as a strategy for maintaining the strength of the local before the inexorable spread of the global. In other words, local (or national) culture claims a new validity to resist impingement by global homogenization. More than anything else, this resistance explains the growing power that culture rights and rights of self-determination exercise within the wider discourse of human rights. Traditional group attachments and connections seem most threatened by globalization, and to protect the right of individuals to enjoy their own culture, it becomes clear that what really needs protection is the group's right to persist *as* a culture. Human rights therefore present a competing universalist principle to protect local or national cultures from the impact of globalization, but it is the human rights of groups, not individual persons, for which the claim to universality is strongest.

It is within this context of global and local, and of group and individual rights that environmental human rights has a major leadership role to play in negotiating the competing yet wedded pressures of globalization and local culture. Environmental human rights are both a metaphor for this dialectical struggle and a policy area within it. In my opinion, environmental human rights are an efficacious place to start in the mediation of global effects on local cultures. Environmental rights are intrinsically group rights, and they empower local cultures both for the immediacy of environmental resources that a culture controls and for the global effects that emanate from how a society uses the resources under its stewardship.

GLOBALIZATION AND ENVIRONMENT AS EMERGENT PHENOMENA

Eleanor Roosevelt first noted the global/local structure of belief in human rights in a United Nations General Assembly Speech in 1958:

> Where after all, do universal rights begin? In small places, close to home – so close and so small that they cannot be seen on any map of the world. Yet they are the world of the individual person: the neighborhood he lives in; the school or college he attends; the factory, farms or office where he works. Such are the places where every man, woman, or child seeks equal justice and equal opportunity, equal dignity without discrimination. Unless these rights have meaning there, they have little meaning anywhere.

This much-quoted passage has been invoked in support of arguments for economic rights, women's rights, the rights of children, and a host of other rights of everyday life. Its invocation today, however, keeps us from forgetting in this time of globalized human rights institutions and actors that human rights exist to protect the small and private spaces within individual lives. Globalization makes us seek to protect the secure connections of our local "homes," all the while recognizing that those homes "cannot be seen on any map of the world."

Globalization is seen by many, particularly by those who fear it, as the ultimate emergent phenomenon. As discussed in Chapter 2, emergent phenomena challenge many ideas and predispositions within liberal societies, especially those, such as the United States, that are so predicated on individual concepts of liberty, responsibility, and causation. Emergent phenomena resist explanation or prediction in individualistic terms, because they presume that some ontological effects emerge only at the level of groups and group behavior. To the individual person seeking explanation of events solely in terms of individual events, decisions, or actors, emergent events therefore seem somehow alien, mysterious, and vaguely uncontrollable, and therefore threatening as well. They appear not to be the products of individual choice or decision; therefore they challenge liberal notions of free will and individual agency, on which all other liberal concepts like liberty and responsibility are constructed.

For my purposes in discussing globalization and the natural environment as emergent phenomena, it is not necessary to adopt such a stringent definition of what emergent means. I shall simply approach them both as containing elements for which it is not fruitful for explanatory purposes to deny their emergent character. I shall not insist on the more strict ontological position that reduction to individual events, actors, or decisions is in fact impossible. For instance, it is certainly the case that the global effects of every actor in a particular field – say, financial investment – might be traceable by discovering and summing the decisions of every individual financial officer or institution around the world, but what would be the point for either understanding how global investment operates or for making policy concerning it? The global effects of all investment policies are nevertheless real and felt as such regardless of whether all actors and their actions are identified. Similarly, global climate change is a real, tangible, and measurable phenomenon, no matter how many of its deniers claim that the weather in their towns is clearly too cold to accept the reality of a warming world.

What makes globalization and environmental change seem so daunting for their emergent ontological characteristics is not only that they challenge individualist (or reductionist) concepts of explanation but also of justification. Much of moral theory in general is predicated on the ideas of individual agency and responsibility, and certainly human rights as a system of moral ideas participates in that understanding of morality. For many, however, such as Frank Garcia (1999), globalization denies the basic principle of human rights that individual persons have moral claims that "must be morally and legally prior to society and state" (p. 25). As Nneoma Nwogu (2007) points out, such a belief requires (and as Garcia insists) that in response to globalization, institutions of globalization must all be reconfigured to "prioritize the human rights principle," rather than allowing instead merely the "incorporation of human rights imperatives *into* such institutions (p. 346; emphasis added). Those institutions, however, such as global financial ones, can treat claims from individuals only as citizens of states, because it is as citizens that they make claims. When states themselves do not recognize the human rights of their own citizens, global institutions have little recourse than to follow the states' lead. It might be possible in such cases to work to incorporate human rights imperatives into global institutions by means of the states, but because doing so relies first on individual states recognizing the human rights of their own citizens, only the states themselves can "prioritize" human rights as a moral principle.

When it comes to the environment, the issue of how its emergent nature affects human rights is somewhat different. Because the natural environment has intrinsic emergent properties in terms of its ecological connection of all its parts and encompassing all individual creatures within it, human rights that pertain to environmental effects will have certain emergent aspects as well, some of which we have discussed in Chapter 3. What I want to stress here is that in relation to globalization, those effects are manifested as environmental human rights claims of a particular society and culture, not of the individual citizens within it. These claims (e.g., as evidenced in individual nation's positions in response to Kyoto) involve both claims of national identity and of material self-determination.

Although the human natural environment is of course global, each society (and sometimes separate indigenous cultures within its borders) considers *its* natural environment to be that which extends to its own borders, and in relationship to which aspects of national identity are defined. All nations define their character at least partly in terms of their physical environment, and this fact is important because this is so that environmental human rights can be seen as the birthright of citizens in individual states, although that inheritance might vary widely in different countries. In the United States, the existence of a frontier is sometimes considered a definition of its national identity in earlier centuries, but even with diminution of the western frontier today, the idea of "room to move" and wide open spaces still exerts a palpable tug on U.S. citizens' psychological image of their nation's unique environmental footprint.

Something similar could be said of every nation of course: from the "Emerald Isle" to the beaches of Spain and south to the essentiality of the Nile and to the Outback of Australia. Every nation takes a portion of its self-definition from its unique environmental characteristics and its historic relations to them. Furthermore, within societies indigenous groups might maintain their own and widely different environmental self-definitions, for instance, Native Americans in the United States and Aborigines in Australia. These might become competing self-images relevant both for environmental policy making and for maintenance of culture rights or self-determination claims of indigenous groups.

My point is that some of the most significant "emergent" aspects of the physical environment have to do with how environment constructs national self-image or "character." In other words, the natural environment plays a significant role in national identity. This is a major reason for why global legislation for environmental sustainability is so difficult to enact – different environmental aspects have different cultural effects on different nations and on their national psyches, so a "one-size-fits-all" set of regulations of water or land use is unlikely to be received similarly across different cultures.

Because of their invocation of national identity, environmental rights in important ways function within individual national (or subnational) communities as culture rights. As such, environmental rights are jealously protected by individual cultures or nations with the fervor that comes from a historic self-image partly defined by that environment within its borders and by the mythology built around it. Protecting that culture right therefore means that every nation claims sovereignty over its own determinations as a society about environmental regulations. Those regulations inevitably are viewed then also for their impact on the future generations of *that* culture, but not necessarily of all cultures. For example, we could envision an argument that the Nile is "of Africa," or "of Egypt"; therefore it is for "we Egyptians and Africans" to determine how to preserve it for those (Egyptians and Africans) who come after us.

It should be clear then how the cultural aspects of every nation's environmental heritage lead it to view environmental protection as its own local prerogative (with admittedly global consequences). This means that the cultural right of environmental stewardship readily translates into the political rights of either national sovereignty or group self-determination. I shall look specifically at how political rights of self-determination and national sovereignty play into global environmental decision making on the grounds of protecting environmental human rights in the final section of the chapter.

Unlike the political rights of sovereignty or self-determination, there is no analogous and immediately apparent *cultural* right of environmental decision making, but a relatively recent acknowledgment of cultural entitlement exists in the practice of national apologies, in which one nation or its leaders apologizes for its past and present generations' treatment of another nation's citizens: past, present, and with implications for future ones. I want to view this practice as analogous to the practice of acknowledging the *cultural* environmental human rights held by individual nations, cultures, or other identity groups who define their "groupness" at least partly in terms of their historic relationship with the natural environment. Doing so helps us to recognize more clearly the inherently emergent nature of environmental awareness as a part of national or group culture. In the same way that present or future generations of a victimized culture deserve an apology as a culture (as a matter of right) for abominations perpetrated in the past, so too are future generations of each culture entitled – as a group and as a matter of right – to equally difficult, if less symbolic, ministrations on the part of their living citizens today.

NATIONAL APOLOGIES AND ENVIRONMENTAL HUMAN RIGHTS

I have characterized environmental human rights as rights owed to future generations of one's own society as a matter of justice and obligation. Michael R. Marrus characterizes the recent phenomenon of national apologies similarly as "taking responsibility for breaches in transgenerational obligations" (2007, 91).

As stated, I want to draw a parallel between environmental rights and the right to an apology because of the similar logical structure shared by both, as well as for the relative newness of each as an element in contemporary human rights theory and practice. At the same time, I shall call attention to two important differences between national apologies for past injustices and respect for environmental rights as preventing future injustices. As matters of policy, both apologies and respecting environmental human rights invoke the relevance of the passage of time in unique ways compared to other policy areas. Environmental rights go further, however, in actually providing a tangible, material response rather than merely saying, "We're sorry for what we have done."

National or official apologies and making policy respecting environmental human rights both acknowledge that injustices have been done that have had an impact on victims. An initial difference between them, of course, is that apologies reference past victims, whereas environmental human rights invoke future ones (as well as present ones). Both are cross-generational, however, and in this sense acknowledge present culpability for wrongs remembered and regretted. For philosopher Janna Thompson an apology is an element of "reparative justice" that respects the "reparative entitlement" of victims: "the entitlements claimed by the successors or descendants of victims of injustice and the obligations that are thought to be entailed by those claims" (2002, *xi*). The difference for environmental rights as elements of such reparative justice is that the successor generations actually are – and not just thought to be – the victims of environmental injustice perpetrated in the present and the past.

As the future victims of environmental injustice, our descendants are then worthy of a somewhat different "reparative entitlement" than are recipients of apologies as usually offered. Those who stand to inherit our environmental messes are entitled to *action* and not only symbolic public gestures. They have a right to legislation or policy – both of which will likely require some sacrifice on the part of the living – or other decisions on the part of present citizens to protect their environmental rights. Words are not enough; this kind of forward-looking apology must include action.

Several authors point out that as a matter of policy, apologies do not always include such reparative action and that it is often not even demanded. Martha Minow elucidates the paradoxical nature of national apologies that makes this omission possible. Although by its nature an apology for past wrongs cannot expiate past guilt or change what has been done, "in a mysterious way and according to its own logic, this is precisely what it manages to do" (Minow, 1998, 114). Apologies often are accepted by victims as enough, even if objectively not much has changed. That is the paradoxical nature of apologies and perhaps why they have entered so readily into contemporary politics. In a distributive justice sense, apologies do not necessarily carry much tangible benefit, but as an element of the politics of recognition they manage to focus attention on groups and their claims in ways that can have significant appeal to those groups. Apologies have become prominent within politics therefore as politics has focused more on issues of identity. Nevertheless, the second major difference between environmental rights and apologies is the lack of this paradox within the drive to ensure future environmental rights – the living have to do more than be sorry for the environmental damage we have wrought; we must take steps to alleviate it and its future impact on our successors' human rights.

Both official apologies and environmental human rights, however, begin in similarity as elements of a shared moral constraint on national policy. They are about justice in some sense, even if one is more symbolic a gesture of recognition and the other more focused on tangible concerns of distributive justice. Apologies have indeed become a significant part of the practice of human rights around the globe, particularly in the case of public figures and governments. Examples of official apologies abound, including several from Pope John Paul II regarding church culpability in its relations with women, Jews, Nazi Germany, among many others, and apologies from many political leaders of western nations, including many U.S. presidents (except for George H. W. Bush, who once declared "I will never apologize for the United States of America. I don't care what the facts are" (quoted in Marrus, 2007, 77). Special credit goes to Bill Clinton, who through numerous exercises in public repentance seemed truly to master this genre of official public remorse while at the same time leading those who witnessed them to question their sincerity. Many other national leaders have also engaged in the practice, including Soviet President Mikhail Gorbachev, Japanese Emperor Akihito, Australian Prime Minister Paul Keating, South African President F. W. deKlerk, British Prime Minister Tony Blair, and of course, in 1970 West German Chancellor Willy Brandt on his knees on the site of the Warsaw ghetto, apologizing for the Nazi Holocaust.

The list is long, if not endless. Indeed, Graham G. Dodds (2007) has compiled a list of official public apologists spanning several pages and over 200 entries; significantly, all but the first thirteen occurred since 1960. There is disagreement among human rights and international relations scholars over the real significance of national apologies as either an adequate moral response or effective national policy; nevertheless, there is no denying that those who offer them unquestionably see them as aiming at both goals and probably achieving at least a measure of each. Apologies, in other words, have developed an importance within international politics that encourages public figures and national spokespersons to offer them at least as accompaniments to policy. Because of their intrinsic moral content, apologies then unquestionably elevate concepts like justice and human rights into the foreground of the relations between states. Besides the obvious impact on the traditional realist/idealist debate among international politics scholars, such moral language opens the door to other such constraints on policy, including, for instance, a respect for environmental human rights.

More than such gate opening, however, apologies share certain essential features with a concern for environmental human rights that make it clear that as apologies become more prominent in global relations, the protections of these rights will grow as well. After surveying the literature of official apologies, Michael Marrus (2007, 79) notes that complete apologies contain the following features:

1. An acknowledgment of a wrong committed, including the harm that it caused
2. An acceptance of responsibility for having committed the harm
3. An expression of regret or remorse both for the harm and for having committed the wrong
4. A commitment, explicit or implicit, to reparation, and when appropriate, to nonrepetition of the wrong.

Notice here two things: first, the clearly normative nature of all these features, presuming some system of morality at work that leads to the acceptance of each element; and second, how any policy for respecting the environmental human rights of future generations presumes each and every feature as well. The last element of commitment to reparations does not always accompany official apologies of course – and it should to sustain the parallel to respecting future environmental human rights – but, in Marrus's view, without such a commitment the apology itself fails as a "complete" one. Again, words alone are not enough – either for complete apologies or for respecting human rights of all kinds, including environmental rights.

Marrus's list is incomplete in my view, however, because all of the elements focus only on the apologizer and not the recipients of the apology, and because it omits certain features of the relationship between them. In these omissions lie important similarities between apologies and respect for environmental rights. I would add four additional elements, some of which I have discussed already.

First, all apologies invoke a temporal relationship that encompasses both past and future in a specific way. I have briefly explored this relationship before, but its significance should not be overlooked. Apologies presume that past behavior carries impacts that spill over not only into the present but also into the future; therefore, as Marrus says, a promise of nonrepetition of the wrong in the future is an important requisite of a complete apology. Beyond reparations to present generations, a full apology carries with it a promise that is good in perpetuity, to all future generations. The same time span in the opposite direction is more problematic, of course. It is often a matter of some controversy how far "back in time" an apology must extend, as Marrus suggests in discussing Charles Maier's question of "can there be too much memory?" (1993; quoted in Marrus, 2007, p. 85). Going too far back probably results in a "surfeit of memory" that leads to apologizing for past events over which no living person can reasonably be said to be responsible, but it is never the intention of an apology that the promise to the future has any limitation in time – "never again" means *never*.

In respecting the environmental rights of future generations, the situation is somewhat reversed, because the issue of how many future generations can be said to have an environmental rights–based claim on our behavior can be a daunting proposition stifling conservation policy, for example. This is an issue for the next chapter; what is significant here is the logical similarity between such a concern and the concern for the past involved in official apologies.

A second feature of apologies overlooked by Marrus concerns the identification of a set of victims. Marrus's four features characterize only the actions of the apologizer; they say nothing about the nature of the recipient. One of the distinctively new – and controversial – features of apologies as a component of official statement or policy is the identity of the recipients. In most cases, the target of the apology is not simply a number of individual people, but a group of individual people that both defines itself and was defined by the treatment for which it is now due an apology, specifically *as a group*.

The history of oppression includes stories of both already existing groups being targeted for malign treatment as well as groups being more or less created or identified by the oppressors specifically for the purpose of becoming objects of oppression, or later as recipients of apologies. Many subnational, ethnic, or indigenous groups meet the first definition, but as examples of the latter consider Pope John Paul II's apologies to Galileo and other "truth seekers," to all women for past treatment by the church, and to victims of sexual abuse by priests. In such apologies there is more than an acknowledgment of group identity shared by a set of victims; it is a postulate of identity not necessarily shared by all members of the groups it identifies. It is conceivable that some scientists, women, or sexual abuse victims might be surprised to find themselves part of a group with its own characterization.

Such surprise notwithstanding, it is clear that apologies operate on an ontological level very similar to that of concern for the environmental inheritance of future generations. Both invoke groups in their collective identity as recipients of either rights or apologies, and in some cases the group indicated might be somewhat "abstract." Future groups are obviously abstract, as discussed in Chapter 3, but so too are groups identified by official apologies, even in some sense traditional groups such as those defined by race. I do not want to engage the current debate over the foundation of race to imply that racial groups (receiving apologies) are not genetically determined and therefore not as "abstract" as groups of future citizens who not yet born. The fact remains, however, that in some cases members of the group receiving the apology might not even consider themselves as having that group identity and might even want to deny it to avoid the status of victim. What is important is that apologies, like environmental rights, presume that group identity is important in the assignment of the right to the apology.

From the standpoint of human rights practice, of course, the fact that most official apologies target a group of recipients worthy of concern fortifies a current movement within both the theory and practice of human rights to establish group rights as real – and just as real as individual rights. It is also not my purpose here to enter this ongoing debate, but as established as the practice of official apologies has become, it is certainly clear that the status of groups having claims worthy of recognition by apologies advances the idea of group rights rather far. This is the third omission of Marrus's conception of complete apologies – he neglects to say that what is being acknowledged in the apology is a violation of the victims' *rights*.

It might be possible to construe whichever damage that is being apologized for as not one that violated actual human rights, although quite frankly it is difficult to come up with an example that would suffice. Most official apologies concern treatment such as murder, displacement, torture, denial of due process, or other assaults on the victims' persons, sense of identity, property, or liberties. All of these are amply elaborated on as rights with the UDHR and other documents, so denying that they are actual rights invokes a philosophical position (like utilitarianism) ontologically opposed to rights more than it does any legal or political sense of rights.

More likely, to dispute or mitigate the effect of official apologies in sanctioning group rights, it would be more efficacious to deny that these previously mentioned rights belong to the *group* of victims rather than primarily to its individual members. Fair enough, but the right to the apology itself is one bestowed on the group, and individual recipients receive the apology (and whichever reparations might be attached) only to the extent that they can prove their group identity. Therefore, even if apologies do not necessarily make moot all such philosophical arguments concerning the reality of group rights, they at least add one very important group right to the political mix. In so doing they exhibit their sanguinary nature to the environmental human rights of future generations – and strengthen thereby both the philosophical and political ontology of the latter rights.

Finally, Marrus's list of the four features of apology fails explicitly to name justice as the goal of the apology, or injustice as the wrong that has been perpetrated. This might be mere oversight, because elsewhere in the same piece he discusses approvingly Janna Thompson's attribution of "reparative justice" as the goal of apologies, and furthermore it is clear from his use of the terms "harms" and "wrongs" that he is at least embracing the normative thrust of all apologies.

Naming justice as the goal is, I believe, important if an apology is to have the desired effect, however. As we discussed in Chapter 3, what makes justice distinctive as a moral concept is, as Aristotle first noted and Hume solidified, its requirement of reciprocity as an essential part of the relation it posits between people. Apologies must have this presumption of reciprocity to achieve the desired level of sincerity and to be accepted as meaningful or have their intended effect. In other words, someone has to "receive" that apology for anyone to take it seriously as at all "reparative" or sincere, and for forgiveness to be extended to the apologizer. When apologies fail or are subject to public criticism, what happens is that their intended recipients, for a variety of possible reasons, refuse to play their reciprocal role in the apology process. Those recipients are in many cases dead – victims of the very behavior for which the apology is being made. If the apology is worthwhile, however, there must be a notion of reciprocity that can still pertain and a group that can play its reciprocal role. There is, of course – it is the reciprocal reception of the apology by the relevant group of survivors and descendants of victims, both now and in the future, that allows the apology to rise to the level of justice. This group – in some cases this *abstract* group – is important for the apology to be acceptable as an instance of justice, because it is the source of reciprocity with the maker of the apology. It is also a group, it should be obvious by now, similar in level of abstraction to the recipients of environmental human rights – that is, one analogously similar to future generations of our society. In this way too, apologies mirror the justice relationship put forward by my argument for environmental human rights.

In this section, I have attempted to delineate that there already exists within human rights theory and practice an analogous model for environmental human rights. The right to an apology is a relatively new development in the world of human rights, and as such still contains several controversial elements that I have explored here. The increasing usage and acceptance of official apologies as part of the process of reparative justice needed, in whichever context it is proposed, portends several things for human rights. It means that the field of human rights is still growing and innovating, and indeed is capable of sophisticated and abstract innovation. Second, it participates in other ongoing developments within the theory and practice of human rights, such as the engagement with the phenomenon of group identity and the effects of globalization. Third, it anticipates, at least analogously, an argument for environmental human rights, even when those rights are attached to abstract groups like future generations.

THE RIGHT OF SELF-DETERMINATION AND GLOBAL ENVIRONMENTAL JUSTICE

If the last section sought an analogous argument for environmental human rights, this concluding section seeks a more concrete one emerging from the still-controversial right of self-determination. This right has been proclaimed many times in General Assembly speeches since the United Nations was established and obliquely referred to in foundational human rights documents, including Article 21, section 3 of the UDHR, which announces that "[t]he will of the people shall be the basis of the authority of government." Self-determination as a right, however, has only been explicitly accepted in more recent human rights documents and declarations, including the International Covenant on Civil and Political Rights (ICCPR, 1966), the International Covenant on Economic, Social, and Cultural Rights (ICESC, 1966), the African Charter on Human and People's Rights (1982), the Declaration on the Rights of Persons Belonging to National, Ethnic, and Language Minorities (1992), and the Vienna Declaration and Programme of Action (1993). This right remains a subject of some controversy today, as we shall see; indeed, Jan Klabbers (2006) argues that self-determination is better viewed as legal norm or principle rather than an actual right. As either right or norm, however, its relation to environmental human rights is logical and evocative of arguments that I have made for environmental rights in previous chapters.

Self-determination was first recognized as a principle of international relations in the nineteenth century, coming into common usage, Hannum (1998, 1) declares, as "a principle that first allowed disparate people who spoke the same language, such as Germans and Italians, to group themselves together and form a new state." The principle also "provided a guiding principle or rationale for dismembering the defeated Austro-Hungarian and Ottoman empires." (Hannum, 1998, 1). Recognition of self-determination as an actual right began with the establishment of the United Nations and the UDHR and took on a particular cast within the ICCPR and ICESC as a response to colonialism and the demands for ex-colonials to declare their independence. It has only been in the past 25 years, Hannum argues (1998, 1), that the principle has taken on its current (and controversial) manifestation as declaring "the right of every people – defined ethnically, culturally, or religiously – to have its own independent state."

In this third phase of the right of self-determination, its meaning has been particularly fraught with and subject to legal and philosophical dispute. Today the right is unquestionably perceived, as it has been by the International Criminal Court (Parker, 2000, 1), as a "right held by people rather than a right held by governments alone." As such, self-determination has been adopted by minorities and indigenous peoples as a claim to which they are entitled, even to the extent of defending the right of secession. Here many scholars diverge either in their acceptance or in their interpretation of the right, with well-known defenders of indigenous peoples' rights like Will Kymlicka (1989) and Allen Buchanan (2003) claiming that the right does not extend to secession but to the group's capacity for self-rule in some areas, as well as including some degree of exemption from outside interference or legal proceedings. Klabbers (2006) simply denies that the right could even contain as much as Kymlicka and Buchanan say that it does and still be accepted by any international court or organization. Klabbers concludes instead that claims of self-determination invoke at best a procedural right of members of a group "to see their position taken into account whenever their futures are being decided" (p. 189). For Klabbers, this is really a restatement of a right to participate in democratic decision making, and specifically within that process "the right to be taken seriously."

Despite disputes over the exact content or extent of the right, self-determination is unquestionably a claim made by and also recognized as pertaining to groups – or peoples, however defined. As such, the right of self-determination is intrinsically and immediately suspect within international law. This suspicion is inevitable, Holder (2006, 6) points out, because treating self-determination as a universal human right presents two controversial claims: "that self-determination is a principle that constrains states in their behaviour within their domestic realm, and not only in their behaviour toward other states and territories *outré-mer*; and that one can coherently include peoples' rights among the universal human rights." As such, the right of self-determination challenges the two underlying principles of modern politics and ontology: state sovereignty and individualism.

Holder accepts (somewhat eagerly) that self-determination challenges sovereignty but argues that individualist ontology is not assaulted thereby if we understand the right correctly as one held universally by all people to participate in group decision making and, more important, in group identity. It is in the latter effort of participation in group identity – not just decision making – that the meaning of the right to self-determination most resembles environmental human rights. Furthermore, because as we have seen group identity includes a strong component of identification with the natural environment, the right of self-determination actually presumes that control over the group's natural resources and environment is part of the actual content of its self-determination rights.

To see clearly how self-determination rights must include environmental human rights held collectively by groups or peoples, we must briefly review the historic and legal arguments for the right to self-determination. There are essentially four arguments, beginning with the original U.N. and UDHR positions on colonialism, democracy, and the right to citizenship. This first modern usage during the 1940s and 1950s had to do with self-determination as an element of rectificatory justice. Oppression during decades (or longer) of colonialism grants its own justification for self-determination as a force of liberation, human equality, and simple humanity, and certainly the principle resonates still, as it did initially, in speeches and documents from the U.N. General Assembly. As a recognized element of justice as reparations for colonialism, however, Hannum is correct that within the United Nations self-determination initially could be recognized only as a principle, not a right. This was necessary, Hannum (p. 2) points out, because if it were proclaimed a right it would "necessarily require the dismemberment of colonial empires; if it had included such an understanding, Britain, France, and Belgium simply would not have adhered to the Charter."

The second argument for self-determination is rooted in rights language, specifically the right to participate in decisions affecting one's own future. This is clearly an egalitarian argument and an expressly democratic one. To the extent that both equality and democracy have become perceived as rights of all people and groups, self-determination also has taken on the claiming power of a right. Since at least the beginning of globalization in the 1970s it has been more or less taken for granted that all nations should move toward democracy as a matter of justice and perhaps even of realpolitik. In this period therefore claims of self-determination as a right have been most often heard and largely accepted as legitimate.

A third argument for self-determination rights is a bit more abstract and invokes the idea that every person has the right to "belong" somewhere as an equal respected by others. In other words, every person has the equal right to be a citizen. As we saw in the last chapter, Hannah Arendt's famous discussion of the effects of "statelessness" on the psyche, even the soul, of human beings in *The Origins of Totalitarianism* (1951) exerts a powerful critique of the place of indigenous peoples like the Jews after World War II. Without the collective right of self-determination that creates a place to be and group with whom to "belong," a stateless person exists as either a "pariah" or "parvenu." The pariah is scorned, excluded, and denied freedom; the parvenu loses dignity and self-respect – and also therefore freedom – in making himself or herself the sniveling sycophant desperate for inclusion. Neither, Arendt devastatingly concludes, can ever be seen or respected as a fellow citizen with dignity and equal human rights. Citizenship therefore presumes the right of self-determination, among many other things; without it no one can be a citizen, for there is no group to which to belong.

Arendt's notion of belonging is an expressly political one; that is, the collective identity she defends as needed and sought as a matter of right by all persons is that of citizen, rather than, say, as a member of a kinship group. The right is explicitly of citizenship in a group also characterized itself by the right of self-determination; in other words, the group cannot be a colony subject to some other country empowered to make decisions for it. This must be the case for Arendt because it is only through the life of active public engagement in decision making on matters that affect one's life that one can become truly free. This can only happen in a free society itself autonomous and sovereign. It is a life she calls the "vita activa" of democratic politics; it is the only life that befits the dignity of human beings, and one for which the protection of human rights must be an acknowledgment.

Arendt's case for the right of self-determination is a strong one precisely because it recognizes the distinctively social nature of human identity, not merely social but political also, in that it requires citizenship. Collective identity is a vital human need, but for Arendt it is achievable only in a democratic life of engagement. The collective identity that alone fulfills this most human of needs therefore must be that of citizen. The right of self-determination most closely resembles environmental human rights here, for both presume a powerful drive for collective belonging, but of a particular kind – political identity.

Holder echoes Arendt's political view of the basic human need for collective identity when she defines the right of self-determination as "a universal human right of persons to make decisions in concert with others as a group and for themselves" (2006, 5). The right of self-determination is, as in Arendt, the right to *do* something together, to make decisions, and not merely share a ceremonial meal or common memories. Seeing self-determination rights as universal is preferable, Holder says, because "it offers a more realistic view of the role of communal decision-making plays in individuals' lives" (p. 7). Self-determination is an expressly political and democratic right, and it grants a special kind of attachment to the group through the act of collective deciding. That kind of group identity is necessarily abstract as well as concrete because it must include members of the group no longer or not yet present. In other words, it is an identity shared with past and future members who together define the "state" or polity to which one belongs. Those members have agency in the life of the group; their interests and concerns are part of the ongoing political discussion. They add to the group identity even though they do not yet exist. In other words, as discussed in Chapter 3, they "reciprocate" in the identity and daily political deliberations of present citizens, making those deliberations decisions of justice – the uniquely political value.

As with issues of environmental justice, in which the environmental rights of future generations have agency and offer reciprocity to the present, Holder and Arendt view the right of self-determination essential to the general political goal of justice. In both cases the identity of future generations and their rights are essential to the identity and rights of present citizens.

Of course, the similarity of self-determination and environmental rights is not entirely abstract, because, as we saw in the last chapter, part of any people's identity is defined by its relationship with the natural environment. Recognizing the rights of future citizens to clean air, water, and soil is therefore an essential part of protecting our mutual group identity. Furthermore, the opportunity and ability to do so is part of what the right to self-determination guarantees. An essential part of the emergent and shared identity of all citizens, which recognition of their right to self-determination delivers, is the protection of their own environmental human rights and those of their future compatriots. That both these rights are universally felt and expressly heightened in a globalized world where individuals seek their local place and communal identity is a foundation for consensus on why both rights are so essential. As such, both rights of self-determination and environmental human rights, but especially the latter, offer an avenue toward global consensus on human rights.

CONCLUSION: GLOBAL CONSENSUS
AND ENVIRONMENTAL REALITIES

As we have seen throughout this chapter, the presumption that globalization naturally leads to consensus on core human rights values and practices is challenged by the somewhat opposite pressure to protect the local amidst the global – to secure one's locality, home, or cultural community as a buffer or protection from the anonymity that a global mass society seems to portend.

That urge to the local can be seen as a threat either to a global consensus on human rights or to the human rights of individual subjects within cultural groups. The right to official apologies is a direct response to that need to protect cultural or group identity, because the recognition that comes with the apology is an acknowledgment of the specialness of group history, suffering, or injustice.

The right to self-determination, conversely, is often criticized for delivering protection for group cultural practices that uphold the local culture while at the same time threatening or violating the human rights of some members of the group. Often those threatened are women – one egregious example being the cultural practice of genital cutting. Both the rights to apology and to self-determination seem therefore to threaten either a global consensus on human rights through their emphasis on cultural difference, or by putting at risk the human rights of a person as individual. If true, this would make the fact that they also resemble environmental rights in some ways simply be too bad for environmental rights, because the latter rights might be tainted by the association. Furthermore, it would be difficult in such a circumstance to argue (as I have) that environmental human rights can be a foundation on which to build a global consensus embracing these and all other human rights.

It is difficult to credit the criticisms of either the right to apology or to self-determination if one is careful to remember what the history and political nature of those rights are. This is particularly true in the case of self-determination rights, the right most often criticized for being at odds with individual rights. First of all, both the history and internal logic of self-determination rights make it clear that they arose historically as a response to colonial oppression. It strains credulity to believe that the right to self-determination held by a cultural group could then legitimate the oppression of individual members of the group. No person or group can claim as a matter of human right the liberty to oppress others, whether the group is a past colonial power or one of its victims. Oppression is the opposite of respect for human dignity; it cannot therefore be behavior protected as a matter of human rights.

Besides, as we have seen, the logic of the right to self-determination is grounded in claims of equality and democratic citizenship, not merely of belonging to a group. Members of groups oppressed by the group's cultural practices are clearly not being treated as equal citizens, nor are they guaranteed the specifically *political* identity and participatory opportunities that this most political of group rights manifests. Women victimized by the social practice of genital cutting might indeed be fulfilling some culturally prescribed role in the group, but it cannot be the role prescribed by the right of self-determination of the group. In fact, in its denial of equal citizenship the practice is itself an abomination of that right.

Although they do not threaten individual human rights, the rights to apologies and to self-determination nevertheless remain ineluctably group rights, and because they do they belong to a special kind of human right that includes the right to a clean environment. All three of these rights seek to maintain the local identity of the peoples they protect, and all presume that that identity is an emergent one that embraces generations past and not yet born. They also all invoke a political argument for justice that is normative in its insistence that what is at stake is a matter of right, and that by protecting the rights of either past or future members of the group, one is also both guaranteeing the rights of present members of the particular group, as well as all similar ones. Because all human beings belong to some such group – we are all of a particular people – agreeing to defend the apology, self-determination, or environmental rights of one people is to defend those rights globally. That sounds like the beginning of consensus, or at least of what Zehra Arat (2006, 424) terms "constructing norms for a global culture."

Finally, one of the impediments to building a global consensus on human rights has not only been the problem that some cultures see human rights as the artifacts only of an alien (read "Western") culture. Agreement on the right of self-determination can go some distance in overcoming this particular point of conflict, but also pertinent is the charge that there is little agreement even between the rights themselves. Do some human rights conflict with others? Can economic or social rights really be achieved without denial of other rights? Do group culture rights not threaten individual rights? Perhaps we need a consensus (or at least a lack of contradiction) among the rights themselves before we can expect a consensus *about* them that can be shared by all cultures.

Although rather abstract, this is an interesting bit of sophistry that must be put to rest, and that much of this chapter's subtext has aimed at achieving. All rights exist logically as claims, of course, so they presume competition if not actual conflict. That is why human rights are political things – they require public deliberation about their applicability or potential conflict in specific circumstances. Because they are human rights that presume the equal dignity of all persons, they also presume that deliberation must be democratic and, as we shall see in the next chapter, guaranteed by constitutions that limit political power. Of course, at the end of the day some decision is made, and one right indeed gives way to another – not everywhere and not forever, but for here, for example in this developing society, and for today, to work toward a different resolution tomorrow.

Even though the logic of rights necessarily means that they will sometimes not be in agreement (consensus?) with each other, it is still important to mark those occasions when rights themselves begin to come together toward common ends. The three rights discussed in this chapter represent that very sort of philosophical convergence, and because they do we should honor the progress they make toward a consensus on human rights across the globe. Environmental rights – even more than the rights to apologies and to self-determination – go furthest in bringing together the apparently disparate concerns of different peoples and different generations. Environmental human rights merge local identity as partially defined by each particular culture's relationship with its environment with a more global identity of all cultures who define themselves the same way. The emerging identity of each culture ultimately is defined by a natural environment that spans all cultures and is therefore intimately bound globally with all other cultural identities and not only in that time and place, but for all future generations of each culture as well. That is the beginning of a global consensus on human rights, initiated by the recognition of the environmental human rights to clean air, water, and soil that all humans, regardless of their locality, can breathe, drink, and till.

6

Human Rights as Inheritance: Instituting Intergenerational Environmental Justice

Thou shalt raise up the foundations of many generations, and thou shalt be called the repairer of the breach, the restorer of paths to dwell in.

Isaiah 58:12

Toward the end of *An Inconvenient Truth*, former Vice-President and Nobel Prize winner Al Gore's movie and book (2006) exposing the prospects of global warming and climate change, Gore concludes that the solutions to environmental degradation lie within reach, but only if there exists enough political will to make difficult policy decisions. The sentiment is somewhat truistic, because the need for sufficient political will is necessary for any decision on many issues facing every nation and every generation. All collective choices wait on the coalescence of political will, so that the issue really depends on how we build sufficient political will to make the necessary environmental decisions that will indeed save the earth. In this book I have argued that employing the language and persuasive power of human rights presents a new, muscular approach to recognizing environmental ethical obligations to future generations. In other words, the power of human rights is uniquely suited to assisting us in gathering the collective will necessary to preserve the planet.

That collective will, I have argued, is distributed within nations and peoples but rarely shared among them. This presents both a particular difficulty of collective action regarding the environment as well as suggesting an alternative path on which to travel in building sufficient political will to confront a global problem. The difficulty is rather obvious – because we are considering a set of global issues when considering the earth's environment, all nations around the world must participate in building political will to confront climate change. That means that every nation and culture with its own unique and different language, ideas, history, traditions, values – its different *politics* – must perform the same tasks and make the same political choices to arrive

117

at the same political will to effect environmental change. At least in terms of political cooperation, overcoming such widespread diversity in service of environmental protection has been extremely difficult.

I have argued throughout this book that a better approach toward arriving at real environmental protection is to rely on the political will already present in every society to protect its own future generations. That will exists as an expression of political community and therefore recognizes as limitations the borders of that community – at least the spatial borders, but we are also especially interested in the temporal borders within which communities exist, because what we are preserving is the planet that future generations will inherit.

That natural inheritance is also a normative one, usually called *environmental justice*, and is preserved by the obligations that the present generation recognizes to the generations coming after. Those obligations are best recognized, enforced, and put into policy within individual political communities, I have claimed, because human identity is uniquely constructed on the strength of our communal attachments. That identity and its attachments mean that as a species we have difficulty recognizing obligations to – as the future generations of other communities invariably are – perfect strangers. The political will to recognize environmental obligations to future generations is, in other words, a communal will. What I have suggested is that the recognition of environmental human rights will place us on the path to gathering the necessary political will *within* each political community as it frames its obligations to its own future generations.

In this chapter we shall explore the political, legal, and institutional manifestations of that gathering will. My focus on individual communities is not meant to ignore either the many treaties uniting nations, communities, and peoples in pursuit of environmental goals, or the various proposals for creating a global political community. Indeed, several treaties have incorporated the language of human rights in service of protecting our environmental legacy, and the next section includes an exploration of some of those international agreements. Similarly, some proposals for global governance specifically bring to bear the democratic concerns that I shall raise in the final section of the chapter, and we shall briefly discuss one of them, David Held's evocative idea of "cosmopolitan democracy" (Held, 1995, 2004, 2006; Held and McGrew, 2007).

The general thrust of my communal approach to respecting human rights clearly leads to low expectations for international cooperation in the service of environmental human rights and environmental protection. The implementation of intergenerational environmental justice using environmental human rights therefore relies on different, mostly national mechanisms. This is not to say that international approaches to both environmental justice and human rights should not be pursued; rather, I shall argue that it is within nations viewed as political communities concerned with their own successor generations that environmental justice finds its impetus. From such local beginnings can international agreements to protect the global environment have the best hope of flowering, if in every community the language of human rights becomes the universal dialect of environmental justice across time and generations.

Intergenerational environmental justice therefore relies on the widespread acceptance across cultures of the language and meaning of human rights, notably environmental human rights, and the incorporation of them into their own respective political institutions. Such a consensus means that for many nations, other changes in political will and its organization by political institutions and procedures must also occur, specifically surrounding the requirement of constitutionalism.

I shall argue in the following sections that incorporating environmental human rights into every political culture to work toward intergenerational environmental justice will also lead to a broadening consensus on the furtherance of human rights as a particular goal of every society. This means that two related developments within the politics of every nation must – and will – follow from the drive to secure every nation's environmental future. The first is that achieving that future requires democracy, and indeed that any political system that truly pursues human rights must also move toward a more democratic mode of political organization and participation. Second, human rights in general, but particularly environmental rights, should be incorporated within every political culture as constitutional rights. I rely somewhat on Tim Hayward's (2005) argument for constitutional environmental rights here, but more heavily on aspects of the argument of the previous chapters. Uniquely among all political institutions, constitutions stipulate a special relationship to the past and future, to past and future citizens, and generally to the concept of time within a political community. Because of that relationship, the endeavor for environmental human rights must include a global drive for the incorporation of constitutional environmental rights within every national political community.

INTERNATIONAL AGREEMENTS AND THE ADDRESSEES OF ENVIRONMENTAL HUMAN RIGHTS

Over the past 30 years, many nations, through a series of agreements, have moved closer to recognizing the right to a safe environment as a legitimate human right. In fact, legal scholar Richard Herz (2000, 58) counts 350 multi-nation treaties and 1,000 bilateral treaties, as well as numerous resolutions among intergovernmental organizations that assert a duty within international law to protect the environment. This does not necessarily mean, however, that environmental human rights are closer to being a legal reality today than before the agreements. We should expect this mixed consequence given the reality of communal and national attachments that characterize both human identity and politics and that has been a major aspect of the discussion of the last two chapters. Those attachments have frequently led to a denial of international obligations on the part even of signatory nations like the United States to agreements such as the Kyoto Protocols. Nevertheless, the sheer number of international documents over the past several decades invoking calls to recognize environmental obligations and even employing the language of human rights in so doing is impressive.

Beginning with a U.N. conference called in Stockholm in 1972, international obligations to protect the environment first became formulated within the language of human rights. The Stockholm Declaration in its first principle stated the following:

> Man has the fundamental right to freedom, equality, and adequate conditions of life, in an environment of a quality that permits a life of dignity and well-being, and he bears a solemn responsibility to protect and improve the environment for present and future generations.

In its employ of both the concepts of dignity and future generations, the Stockholm Declaration, although itself nonbinding on its 114 signatory nations, clearly paved the way for a variety of subsequent declarations proclaiming both individual environmental human rights and national obligations for environmental justice for both present and future generations.

For instance, The African Charter of Human and Peoples' Rights (1981) includes Article 24: "All peoples shall have the right to a general satisfactory environment favourable to their development." The African Charter's invocation of "people's rights" led to significant discussions within the human rights community on the new topic of "group rights," as noted in the previous chapters, but it was also the first time that a specific "right to a favourable environment" was named in international documents.

In 1987, the report of the U.N. World Commission on Environment and Development (WCED) issued its report, "Our Common Future," better known by the name of its chair, Gro Harlem Brundtland. Coining the term "sustainable development" and characterizing it as "development that meets the needs of the present without compromising the ability of future generations to meet their own needs," the Brundtland Report did more than firmly establish environmental protection as essentially an issue of intergenerational justice, although it certainly did that. It also, as Tim Hayward (2005, 55) notes, "presented the basic goals of environmentalism as an extension of the existing human rights discourse." The report states, "All human beings have the fundamental right to an environment adequate for their health and well-being" (WCED 1987, 348).

Also of note, in the U.N. Convention on the Rights of the Child (UNCRC), a treaty Hayward (p. 55) observes as "almost universally ratified," its Article 24 stipulates a child's right "to the enjoyment of the highest attainable standard of health," and (in paragraph c) admonishes signatories that this right requires that they "combat disease and malnutrition, including within the framework of primary health care, through, inter alia, the application of readily available technology and through the provision of adequate nutritious foods and clean drinking water, taking into consideration the dangers and risks of environmental pollution." Like the Brundtland Report, the UNCRC, by focusing on the rights of children, brings to the idea of environmental human rights a clear focus on future generations, thereby linking the idea of environmental human rights with the goal of intergenerational justice.

Finally, in extending the focus on the environmental human rights of groups or peoples, the U.N. Sub-Commission on the Prevention of Discrimination and Protection of Minorities reaffirmed, according to Hayward (p. 56), "a conception of human rights and the environment which captures the spirit of the Principle 1 of the 1972 Stockholm Declaration." The Report of the Sub-Commission, known as the Ksentini Report (1994), included a set of "Draft Principles on Human Rights and the Environment," in which its first principle declares "human rights, an ecologically sound environment, sustainable development and peace are interdependent and indivisible." Although such postulated interdependence and indivisibility might be said to ignore myriad potential conflicts between human rights in general and economic development, in its second principle the Declaration avers that "all persons have the right to a secure, healthy, and ecologically sound environment." Furthermore this right is to be viewed as indistinguishable from other human rights in terms of force or coverage: "This right and other human rights, including civil, cultural, economic, political, and social rights, are universal, interdependent, and indivisible" (p. 75).

The Sub-Commission's Draft Principles merge the twin foci on future generations' rights and on groups and in so doing lay the groundwork for the argument I have made throughout this book, namely, that environmental rights must be seen primarily as a group right, and especially as the rights of future groups. Ironically, however, because it is an addendum to a report about minority groups, the list of environmental rights that constitutes the bulk of the draft mostly uses the language of individual "persons" rather than of groups or "peoples" in its enumeration of environmental rights. Representative are the following from Part I:

- All persons have the right to a secure, healthy, and ecologically sound environment.
- All persons have the right to freedom from pollution, environmental degradation, and activities that adversely affect the environment.
- All persons have the right to safe and healthy food and water adequate to their well-being.
- Everyone has the right to benefit equitably from the conservation and sustainable use of nature and natural resources.

Only rarely do statements that invoke individuals *in groups* appear in the document, and except for one notable exception, such references appear in Part IV, where obligations raised by environmental rights are discussed.[1]

This continued reliance on the individualist language of rights even in a document aimed at the protection of specific groups is noteworthy for a variety of reasons relating to the current status of non-Western, group-oriented approaches to rights that we discussed in earlier chapters. As I shall discuss in the last section of this chapter, in later U.N. environmental documents such as the Aarhus Convention (2001) and the Kiev Protocol (2003), the individualist language in support of environmental rights is continued to make an argument for procedural environmental rights. The reason for this is obvious within the twentieth-century history of human rights, but this inability to move away from a strictly individualist focus also strengthens the most important impediment to instituting environmental human rights within the current rights regime.

Except for some notable exceptions like the African Charter, virtually all international human rights declarations, charters, documents, and so forth invoke the individualist language of the rights of "persons." The reason for this has been historically understandable: besides their grounding in the Western liberal rights tradition, the addressees of human rights are the sovereign states within which individual citizens live and have their rights either protected or violated. Thus, states (as signatories) and their governments promise (or at least state their intention) to protect whichever rights of the individual person

[1] The exception is Number 14 of Part II: "Indigenous peoples have the right to control their lands, territories and natural resources and to maintain their traditional way of life. This includes the right to security in the enjoyment of their means of subsistence."

are the focus of the document. Because states and their representatives have historically resisted admitting, for sovereignty reasons, the existence of indigenous (usually oppressed) "groups" that have separate identities from those of other citizens of the state, the idea of recognizing the rights of members of such groups as "group rights" has been resisted as well. When group rights have been embraced as a concept, such as in the African Charter, the addressee of the rights has also, although somewhat imperceptibly, been altered to refer to either the "international community" or the "parties to the present charter" (Articles 20 and 21). In such cases the rights themselves assume a rather translucent character, because enforcement of them is rendered illusory at best. If individual states will not enforce them, how exactly can the international community or the Organization of African Unity do so, given the absence of sovereignty within either group?

Since the UDHR was first delivered to the world, the protection of human rights has been the responsibility of sovereign states, who often (but not always) recognized human rights as the rights their own citizens were entitled to *because of their citizenship, not their humanity,* and in some cases were already incorporated into a constitution. As the respondents or addressees of human rights within international politics, states clearly defined the holders of human rights as individual persons, particularly their own individual citizens. International disputes often centered on whether other states were living up to their duties regarding the human rights of their own citizens, but very rarely were other nations, or the international community as a whole, ready to step into the role of addressee of those rights to protect them. Doing so would mean intervention of some type into the domestic politics of states, something no human rights document has incorporated into its text. Intervention secondarily usually also carried with it an imputation that some particular group within a country was the victim of rights violations of its members, and that the oppression was predicated on group identity.

Of course, the most apparent instance of group rights violations is the perpetration of genocide, a term created in the twentieth century to distinguish it as a different crime (that "had no name" in Churchill's famous phrase) from large-scale murder, a crime recognized by every legal code. Genocide has become accepted as the violation of a group right, but except for the related violation of ethnic cleansing, no other group right has received widespread acceptance throughout the international community or within its member states.

The reasons for this reluctance are too many and complex to visit here, but it is important to see just how environmental human rights bridge the gap between the original excessively individualist formulation of human rights in older documents such as the UDHR, and the newer, group-rights focus

of the Convention Against Genocide and the African Charter. It is in their
embrace of both types of approaches that environmental human rights offer a
way forward in the further incorporation of human rights into all national and
international politics.

Put simply, environmental human rights are group rights that nevertheless
retain the same addressee of individualist human rights: individual states and
the communities they represent and protect. As I have formulated them, environmental rights belong first to living people both as individual persons and
as members of communities; in this formulation their holders are noncon-
troversial because most human rights are presumed to be individual rights.
Environmental human rights are unique, however, as I have claimed, in that
they also belong to future generations as group rights. I have also argued that
for both philosophical reasons having to do with the nature of human identity
and for practical reasons, it makes sense to view the group holders of environmental rights as the future generations of (every)one's own community, rather
than of all future persons.

The group nature of environmental human rights would seem to invoke
a different protector or addressee of these rights, especially given the global
character of the environment itself and the current environmental issues we
face, such as global warming. Thus we would expect that international bodies
such as the United Nations or international courts would be the locale for the
protection of environmental human rights. Because I have argued that these
rights should be recognized as those of one's own national community – both
its present citizens and the group of its future generations – it is clear that
the burden of protection would be maintained within the institutions of one's
own sovereign state. In other words, as with all human rights, environmental
human rights – although constituting a group right when applied to future
generations – presume that sovereign states remain their addressees.

The significance of retaining the present understanding of the addressee
of human rights when promoting the new right to clean air, water, and soil
should be evident, at least in a practical sense. Most human rights theorists, practitioners, activists, and international bodies still agree with James W.
Nickel, who states (2002, 358), "one's own country remains the addressee of
one's Human Rights, and one's legal system remains the primary forum for
dealing with alleged violation of one's rights." Because environmental human
rights maintain this traditional (although not uncontroversial[2]) relationship of
human rights to sovereign states several consequences follow.

---

[2] Both Nickel and Alan Gewirth deny that nations and their governments are the *only* addressee
of human rights. See Nickel (2002), and Gewirth (1996).

First and most obviously, in a pragmatic sense it is easier to argue for a new kind of right without also having also to argue for an entirely new system of enforcement. Although environmental rights by their nature do not rule out international cooperation in pursuit of their protection, and in some cases might even encourage a voluntary transfer of authority from national institutions to international ones, the fact that the primary addressee remains one's own government in its duty to protect the rights of future citizens makes the realm of political action a familiar one. Of course, the protection of those rights might even constitute an argument for why on some environmental issues the duty of one's national government – the addressee of one's rights – *must* transfer its authority at least temporarily to an international body. If only an international body can respond to an issue such as, for instance, the melting of the polar ice cap, then present and future citizens have a right to the transferral of addressee authority to such a body.[3]

As Ovadia Ezra (2008) points out, the issue of who is the addressee of human rights "inserts an essentially political component into the concept of human rights" as a necessary counterpart to its morally universalist aspect. These two components of human rights – their universal and political sides – are often in tension or even in contradiction whenever violations of human rights occur. Rights are taken to be universally applicable but locally applied, in other words. When violations occur, it is often the local addressee – one's sovereign state government – behaving in a way that violates rights understood to be universal. Ezra uses as his example of an instance of such apparent contradiction Nickel's (2002) discussion of presidential emergency powers restricting human rights in the name of national security, but protecting environmental rights is another efficacious example.

Violations of environmental rights place the universality of such rights into special conflict with their political implementation, because it would seem that acting alone, no single nation or political unit can solve global climate change, for example. Environmental rights therefore would seem to be logically impossible unless the addressee for these rights were to change. I want to argue, however, that given whose rights are being protected, keeping sovereign nations as the addressee of such rights is the only way to guarantee their protection. Furthermore, the essential step in providing that guarantee is emphatically not to transfer authority to an international body – at least not permanently, but to more deeply institutionalize environmental human rights into the politics of each nation. Doing so requires two steps: first, the protection

---

[3] I am grateful for this example to Ovadia Ezra (forthcoming in **Journal of Human Rights**), "Human Rights: The Immanent Dichotomy."

of environmental human rights, given their dual set of holders, requires a constitutional sanction. Therefore, environmental human rights should be written into every national constitution. The reasons for this requirement are explored in the next section.

Second, the politics of environmental human rights – essential, and essentially national as it is – must be open to all citizens. This is another way of saying that in addition to the substantive rights to clean air, water, and soil, environmental human rights include procedural rights as well; that is, they presume that the right of free and unhindered citizen participation in environmental policy making be held equally by all citizens. Included also are the procedural environmental rights of future citizens, who must be granted a unique form of political standing to guarantee their participation in environmental policy. As will be discussed in the last section of this chapter, environmental human rights – particularly the procedural right to participation – therefore presume and require democratic decision making.

CONSTITUTIONALISM AND THE RIGHTS OF THE FUTURE

National constitutions often include, as in the U.S. case, a list of individual rights that the government being described in the document is charged to protect, but constitutions need not necessarily include such a list of rights. It is possible, again as in the U.S. case, for the rights to be named and included later as a series of amendments. It is even possible that a constitutional government can be erected and sustained without a written constitution, as is the case in Great Britain, nor is it necessary or even common that any list of constitutional rights would include environmental rights, although, by Donald K. Anton's count (1998), more than fifty national constitutions do include language referring either to expressly stated environmental rights or to state obligations to protect the environmental heritage of present and future generations. One of the oldest national constitutions – that of the United States – not only does not include an environmental right in its famous Bill of Rights but also can be interpreted (Lazarus, 2004, Ch. 3) as being one of the most opposed to its inclusion.

In this section, I shall argue that an important step in the implementation of environmental human rights and intergenerational environmental justice is the incorporation into every national constitution of the environmental human right to clean air, water, and soil. Other scholars (cf. Hayward, 2005; Nedelsky, 2008) have very recently begun to make the same plea, but the argument I shall make diverges significantly from theirs in its drawing on the communal, relational, and intergenerational aspects of both human identity and of rights that I have developed in preceding chapters.

What makes constitutional rights special goes beyond their politically pragmatic value in restricting the power of government to take action or to legislate on any issue it wishes. All constitutions so limit governmental power, of course, but as constitutional elements, enumerated rights present a uniquely intergenerational and relational picture of the community *across time*; that is, as a collection of people who share a set of values and identity that makes them recognizable as fellow citizens no matter how far separated by the passage of time. As such, constitutions have a unique role to play in the protection of environmental rights, whose implementation and enforcement require that same sense of the connection of citizens across generations.

As preparation for this argument, we must first briefly explore the general nature of constitutions and constitutionalism. It is commonly accepted that constitutional government is characterized by a few basic elements. First, limitation – all constitutional governments are intrinsically limited governments; that is to say, constitutional governments are restricted in the number and extent of the actions they may take in relation to citizens. Second, as first and perhaps best formulated by John Locke, the legitimacy of the authority of constitutional governments is expressly bound up in the extent to which they observe those limitations. Third, the limitations on government that define its constitutional character are under the active purview of its citizens; that is, citizens (or their representatives) are ultimately the ones with the constitutional authority to limit government's action under the aegis of their role as the "creators" through consent of government itself. Constitutional government is assumed to be an artifact of human (citizen) creation. It is this last assumption that marks constitutionalism as a distinctly modern political doctrine, dating back only to the seventeenth century.

It is the third element of constitutionalism that accounts for its amenability to ideas of inalienable citizen rights, even to the extent of incorporating an enumeration of those rights within the written constitution itself. These rights represent the protections supplied by the mechanism of constitutional limitation on government, whether they are taken in the U.S. sense of being explicitly "individual" rights, or construed as broader rights of the community itself. It is nevertheless conceivable that constitutionalism (and constitutional governments) could exist without the idea or inclusion of individual rights. Logically as well as traditionally, beginning with the U.S. Constitution's acknowledgment of "inalienable" rights and extending into the present era's trumpeting of "human" rights, rights and constitutionalism have become wedded in most observers' minds as the most common and efficacious method of governmental limitation.

The role of rights within constitutional systems also highlights a fourth element of most constitutions: they are collective statements of a nation's values, character, or identity. Not all constitutions are the same, obviously, but their differences ultimately indicate cultural differences between national communities who see themselves as unique. In my view, this cultural identity aspect of constitutions is crucial to understand, because it is what makes citizens recognize themselves and each other across time as fellow members of the same community.

Constitutions define the borders of a nation by demarcating what persons within those borders share in terms of their political beliefs and values. Anyone living within those borders can thus be recognized as "one of us," no matter whether that person lived 200 years ago or has yet to be born. Obviously, people live and die, but nations continue and citizens recognize each other as fellow nationals over the course of hundreds of years. Why? Because they share the same beliefs, values, and principles as enumerated (in written form or not) in their shared constitution. Constitutions provide much of the tradition that binds individual citizens into a community with a recognizable past and future, and therefore a shared identity that is rooted both in stories of the past and in an anticipated future. Communal traditions, in other words, make citizens remember not only the past but also the future in the sense of being cognizant of their responsibilities toward future citizens. Politically, constitutions provide this link across time that connects all citizens both to their enduring governmental institutions and to the community they share with all past and future citizens.

Concretely, of course, the constitutional "matter" that persists over time is the fundamental structure (i.e., divisions, branches, offices) of government and society as often described in the constitution. In the U.S. Constitution, most of the pages are given over to this description of the political institutions that define what the United States of America will look like politically and that are expected to continue to exist – in possibly amended form – into the distant future. Even in this seemingly descriptive role, however, the impact of a nation's constitution on the symbolic and psychological life of society should not be ignored. It is often the case that the line between the "concrete" matter of constitutionalism and its symbolic content in terms of shared values and national identity is not very clearly drawn. For instance, it is deeply embedded in the U.S. consciousness that who we are is inextricably tied to our belief in free and frequent elections, free speech guarantees, or a distinctive separation and balance of powers between and within levels of government.

The fifth function that constitutions fulfill is providing this description of the structures of governmental process. Of course, as in the U.S. case, clarity in this constitutional function is a relative thing, and perhaps intentionally so, as the framers might purposively leave details concerning political processes to be filled in later as society changes and political practices evolve. Also, following the U.S. example, most constitutions include clauses describing the process by which they might be amended.

In both cases of intentional constitutional vagueness and providing procedures for amendment, constitutions relate an important truth about political society that is directly relevant to our consideration of environmental constitutional rights. Political society is composed of relationships among citizens and between citizens and their government. Those relationships might evolve and change over time, but their basic structure must be demarcated and protected by the national constitution itself. Furthermore, when citizens act politically it is assumed that they do so with these relationships ever present in their minds, so that their actions at the very least do not violate constitutional definitions of political behavior or constitutionally defined protection of other citizens' constitutional roles. Because the constitution presumes the relation of past, present, and future generations of citizens, those considerations of the effects of present behavior take on one additional element: the twin caveats of respecting the past and preserving the future.

Because of all its many impacts on the life and future of political society, the national constitution is clearly where the environmental human right must reside. Constitutions construct the relations that are to pertain to a nation's political behavior, including its behavior regarding future generations of citizens. Those relations are partially defined by the rights that are included in the constitution, which are to be understood as themselves defining which relations are permitted among citizens and between citizens and their government. This is arguably true for all rights, because, as Nedelsky (2008) argues, all rights are intrinsically relational in nature. Although the often-heard criticism of rights as too "individualist" tends to ignore this reality, the truth is that "what rights in fact do and have always done is construct relationships – of power, of responsibility, of trust, of obligation. Legal rights can protect individuals and the values that matter to them, but they do so by structuring the relations that foster those values. Thus all rights, the very concept of rights, is best understood in terms of relations" (p. 141).

Constitutional rights are particularly relational in Nedelsky's sense, because they intentionally establish long-term relationships that are to govern political, social, and economic behaviors and practices within a country. Among these I would argue (although Nedelsky does not) that environmental rights are uniquely amenable to and deserving of inclusion in constitutions. This is because first, as we have seen in previous chapters, environmental rights more than any others verify the relational aspects not only of rights but also of human identity. Environmental rights call attention to the impact that others have on our own individual lives as well as to the interconnection of all life itself to a degree more than any other right.

Furthermore, environmental rights invoke the presence of the past and of future citizens in an especially intense way, and because they do, therefore they belong in constitutions, the expressed purpose of which is to establish the relations between all generations of citizens with each other and with the foundations of their government. Constitutions are where societies establish the values that are to guide political and social intercourse for generations to come, and also where those values are protected by incorporating them as constitutional obligations or rights. This is especially true in democracies, Nedelsky declares (2008, 153) where constitutions establish "mechanisms of ongoing dialogue about whether the collective choices people make through their democratic assemblies are consistent with their deepest values." There is both a procedural element here within constitutional rights that we will discuss in the next section, as well as a recognition of how even the most dearly held values of a society can be put at risk by democratic decision making. Therefore, those values are established within the constitution as a way both to acknowledge their centrality to a society's self-definition and their openness to alteration or denial, a risk that is always present within democratic politics. Nedelsky concludes (p. 153):

> When a society chooses to constitutionalize a value, to treat it as a constitutional right, they [sic] are in effect saying *both* that there is deeply shared consensus about the importance of that value *and* that they think that value is at risk. The same people (collectively) who value it are likely to violate it through their ordinary political processes. Although an apparent paradox, this duality makes sense. There are lots of values like that. It may be that the fear is that different majorities at different times will be willing to violate rights they care about if the violation primarily affects a minority to which they do not belong. (emphases Nedelsky's)

Nedelsky's defense of constitutional rights is aimed as a response to arguments such as Waldron's (1993), which contend that because all constitutional rights provisions prevent future democratic majorities from taking certain actions that violate those rights, the rights themselves are intrinsically undemocratic. I do not wish to explore this debate completely here (although I will take it up again later in this chapter), except to agree with Nedelsky that democracy includes more fundamental values than that of majority rule, and that those values are properly placed within constitutions. Furthermore, I contend that protecting the environment for future generations of citizens is properly one of those values that deserves to be incorporated as a constitutional right.

As I have already argued, few if any rights invoke the welfare of future generations as insistently as do environmental rights. No other right draws attention as clearly to the interconnection between citizens, to their relationships with the natural environment and how those relationships affect those with other citizens. No other right makes clear the power that the present generation has over the welfare of those that succeed it. The future is always the minority in the eyes of those who control the present. Future citizens have no vote, no recourse against the will of the living majority, and are beyond the bounds of justice *unless* their rights are incorporated into the document that restricts the actions of the living in the name of the rights of the future.

Only environmental human rights invoke the unique relationship with nature that partially defines every nation's self-identity. Because nature is characterized by the irrevocable interconnection of all things dead, living, and not yet born (think compost, plants, seeds), only a constitution, of all of a nation's documents, laws, or institutions, can mirror that same fundamental relationship in its past, present, and future institutions and citizens. As we saw in Chapter 3, only environmental rights offer the reciprocity between future and present that makes intergenerational justice possible, as well as providing a powerful enough – and self-interested enough – argument for the present generation of citizens to limit its environmental impact. Of any right deserving of inclusion into a national constitution, environmental rights are the most appropriate to be found there.

Why in a practical sense is constitutional status so important for environmental rights, even if logically we can see that they are apt additions to any constitution? There are many benefits that accrue from constitutional status that are worth recounting, and especially in the case of environmental rights the last such benefit, because it also speaks to Waldron's misgivings about constitutional rights in general. As both international treaties and constitutional scholars have interpreted them, environmental rights include a procedural element aimed at enhancing their positive effect on democratic practice.

In recounting these benefits, I shall mostly follow the introductory justification for constitutional environmental rights offered by Tim Hayward (2005, 5–8). First, in a legal sense, constitutional provisions carry the greatest clout or "trumping" power over other legislation, administrative rulings, judicial determinations, or political decisions that might weaken environmental laws without constitutional status: therefore, incorporating environmental rights within the constitution "enshrines a recognition of the importance a society attaches to environmental protection" (p. 5).

Second, given the fact that environmental laws and other provisions make up a vast and disparate pastiche of regulations concerning air pollution, water quality, dumping provisions, impact statements, and a variety of other policy areas, "constitutional provisions can promote the coordination of environmental protection measures with a jurisdiction" (p. 5). Third, in societies like the United States, where individual states have considerable responsibility and authority over their own land areas, a constitutional provision for environmental rights can "also serve to promote the coordination of environmental protection measures between states" (p. 5). Clearly such coordination is indicated by the nature of environmental issues themselves, which for the most part do not honor state boundaries.

Fourth, constitutional provisions for environmental rights function to restrain actions by narrow (or narrow-minded) majorities that might be deleterious to long-term environmental protection, while at the same time (and fifth) encouraging environmental participation on the part of citizens. As Hayward points out, it is often the case that slim legislative majorities (in both state and national legislatures) might be tempted by short-range electoral concerns to avoid difficult decisions necessary to protect environmental rights of future citizens. Doing so would be considerably more difficult if those rights were under constitutional protection.

Finally, and in partial response to the concern expressed by Waldron about the anti-democratic nature of all constitutional rights, constitutional environmental rights would serve to enhance the democratic participation that he fears is always threatened by the prohibitions entailed by any constitutional provision. Waldron is correct that constitutions by their nature take certain decisions out of the hands of any given majority at any given time; for instance, a simple majority of citizens or legislatures cannot alter the tripartite structure of the U.S. federal government. He is also correct that including rights provisions in constitutions makes it impossible for majorities to rescind those rights whenever they might consider it convenient or even necessary to do so (e.g., in wartime). Regardless of whether we consider this a weakness or strength of constitutional rights, however, when it comes to constitutional environmental rights, the overall effect of their implementation would be to increase participation and therefore democratic discussion. This is true for two reasons, as Hayward notes. First, because as we shall see in the next section, virtually all constitutional provisions for environmental rights – as well as most treaties and diplomatic agreements for environmental protection – include strongly worded procedural rights guaranteeing access to information and participation in environmental decisions. Second, the holding of environmental rights, with their procedural guarantees, can serve to educate and motivate citizens to become more active in environmental decisions.

For all these practical reasons having to do with enhancing the political weight of environmental issues and decisions, constitutionally enumerated environmental rights recommend themselves as a crucial first step in the guaranteeing of intergenerational environmental justice. Hayward summarizes these arguments (p. 8):

> In signaling the "trumping" status of environmental concern in relation to lesser obligations of the state, rights provide means for citizens and the associations to challenge the state when it fails to meet its obligations. Giving constitutional force to a right of environmental protection can give this a due weight in the balance with other social values which already have the status of rights, particularly those associated with economic development, rather than being seen as a partisan cause.

Of course, standing behind these practical and political reasons for constitutional environmental rights are the ones discussed earlier that emanate from the shared internal nature of both the environment and of political bodies as emergent, collective phenomena. The logic of the convergence of the natural environment and political communities is such that only the communally based, generationally timeless, identity-defining aspects of a nation's constitution are capable of addressing the environmental demands of future as well as living citizens. Why that logic is also intrinsically a democratic as well as a constitutional one is the issue to which we must now turn.

PARTICIPATORY DEMOCRACY AND INTERGENERATIONAL ENVIRONMENTAL JUSTICE

As stated above, many treaties, constitutional provisions, and international declarations having to do with the environment include clauses guaranteeing the opportunity for citizens to participate in environmental decisions. Participation is not always framed in terms of human rights, as was the case in the Rio Declaration in 1992. Alan Boyle (1996, 43) laments the fact that 20 years after the U.N. Stockholm conference first declared the human right of "life in an environment of a quality that permits a life of dignity and well-being," the authors of the Rio Declaration shied away from employing rights language in their worldwide call to environmental action. Nevertheless, although Boyle is correct about the absence of rights language, that declaration, in strongly normative terms, acknowledged the moral argument in favor of democratic participation in environmental decisions:

> Environmental issues are best handled with the participation of all concerned citizens, at the relevant level. At the national level, each individual shall have appropriate access to information concerning the environment that is held by public authorities, including information on hazardous materials and activities in their communities, and the opportunity to participate in decision-making processes. States shall facilitate and encourage public awareness and participation by making information widely available. Effective access to judicial and administrative proceedings, including redress and remedy, shall be provided. (Principle 10)

Although not invoking rights language, the normative and peremptory tone of this principle makes it clear that whether grounded in human rights or not, as a matter of moral obligation, states owe citizens the opportunity to have a voice in environmental policy.

Two years later, the language of human rights reentered the international understanding of environmental obligations. In the Ksentini Report (1994) Appendix titled "Draft Principles on Human Rights and the Environment," an entire section (Part III) is given to listing the procedural rights that citizens possess in the making of environmental policy to combat climate change. By establishing these rights as essential to good environmental policy, the report recognized the close relationship between democratic practices and protecting the environment. In so doing, the report also incorporated an important distinction into the discussion of environmental human rights that so far has set these rights off from most other human rights. That distinction denotes both a substantive and procedural side to environmental rights. The procedural environmental rights invoked in Part III of the Draft Principles signal a theoretical innovation in human rights thinking heralded by this new convergence between environmentalism and human rights:

15. All persons have the right to information concerning the environment. This includes information, howsoever compiled, on actions or courses of conduct that may affect the environment and information necessary to enable effective public participation in environmental decision making. The information shall be timely, clear, understandable, and available without undue financial burden to the applicant.

16. All persons have the right to hold and express opinions and to disseminate ideas and information regarding the environment.

17. All persons have the right to environmental and human rights education.
18. All persons have the right to active, free, and meaningful participation in planning and decision-making activities and processes that may have an impact on the environment and development. This includes the right to a prior assessment of the environmental, developmental, and human rights consequences of proposed actions.
19. All persons have the right to associate freely and peacefully with others for purposes of protecting the environment or the rights of persons affected by environmental harms.
20. All persons have the rights to effective remedies and redress in administrative or judicial proceedings for environmental harm or the threat of such harm.

By 1998, the democratic practices guaranteed by right in the Ksentini Report were largely incorporated into a major international treaty, the UNECE Convention on Access to Information, Public Participation in Decision-making and Access to Justice in Environmental Matters. Usually known as the Aarhus Convention, after the Danish city in which it was signed, this treaty went into force in October 2001. Signatories include the entire European Community, the United States, Canada, Israel, and parts of Central Asia. The Aarhus Convention focused largely on democratizing interactions between citizens and their governments on environmental matters but also included a unique compliance mechanism. The Compliance Review Mechanism allows citizens to communicate concerns about any state party's compliance (including their own) directly to a committee of international experts empowered to explore the merits of the complaint. "As of May 2007, 18 communications from the public – many originating with nongovernmental organizations – had been lodged with the Convention's compliance Committee (Wikipedia: http://en.wikipeida.org/wiki/Aarhus_Convention).

Two years later, the Kiev Protocol was addended to the Aarhus Convention to guarantee citizens' access and reporting rights specifically in the area of the pollutant release and transfer registers (PRTRs). Signed by most of the original parties to Aarhus, the Kiev Protocol states as its objective, "to enhance public access to information through the establishment of coherent, nationwide pollutant release and transfer registers (PRTRs)" (UNECE, 2007). Such information can act as the source for all citizens to reference in the course of the application of their environmental rights to oversee and report state environmental practices. Finally, at a second meeting of the parties to the protocol, the Almaty Declaration was adopted, urging all signatories to quickly establish democratic practices for engagement of the public in environmental reporting practices.

> We urge all Signatories to speed up their internal processes with a view to ratification of the Protocol by the end of 2007 and to put in place implementing legislation as well as administrative procedures and mechanisms for establishing operational pollutant release and transfer registers in accordance with the provisions of the Protocol. (UNECE, 2007)

Beginning with the Ksentini Report and including the Aarhus, Kiev, and Almaty documents, a consensus on the way forward in dealing with global environmental issues such as climate change was clear: substantive measures including environmental human rights had to be paired with democratic participatory mechanisms that were to be acknowledged as human rights themselves – the *procedural* human rights to participate in environmental decisions. Environmentalism and democracy were increasingly viewed as two sides of the same coin – the new coin of the global environmental realm: environmental human rights. Environmental scholars such as Edith Brown Weiss (1989), Gunther Handl (1992), and James Nickel (1993) agreed: environmental human rights had to be both substantive and procedural. The latter, however, is the area in which the closeness between environmental human rights, intergenerational justice, and democracy would become most apparent.

According to several scholars (cf. Dobson, 1996; Goodin, 1992; Hayward, 2005; Waldron, 1993) the substantive human environmental rights I have been defending do not necessarily presume a democratic decision-making structure. As Goodin (p. 168) comments, "[t]o advocate democracy is to advocate procedures, to advocate environmentalism is to advocate outcomes" (quoted in Hayward, p. 129). Even if Goodin's apparently narrow definition of democracy is accepted, this does not mean, as Hayward responds (p. 130), that there is anything essentially anti- or nondemocratic about substantive environmental rights. Waldron does make the latter claim, however, at least by implication from his general belief that any substantive outcomes that restrict the choices of future generations intrinsically diminish their democratic rights. This would be particularly true, as we have seen, if those outcomes are stipulated as rights within a constitution, which by its nature denies some actions as violating shared principles stated as a matter of right within that constitution.

Waldron's argument can be taken as a critique of constitutionalism generally, or at least of constitutional bills of rights, but mostly he is concerned with a transfer of power "from the people and their admittedly imperfect representative institutions to a handful of men and women, supposedly of wisdom, learning, virtue and high principle who, it is thought, alone can be trusted to take seriously the great issues that they raise," (p. 20). Specifically, it is courts and their judges that he fears, who will "inevitably become the main forum for the revision and adaptation of basic rights in the case of changing circumstances and social controversies" (ibid.). Waldron finds this development particularly offensive, given that "[S]ome of us think that people have a right to participate in the democratic governance of their community. . . . We think moreover that the right to democracy is a right to participate on equal terms in social decisions on issues of high principle and that it is not to be confined to interstitial matters of social and economic policy" (ibid.).

There is certainly ample evidence in our time that courts in the United States have indeed manifested this tendency to replace other democratic modes of decision making, but it is not clear that the reason they have done so is because democratic constitutions have placed interpretation of rights beyond the reach of any political process other than a judicial one. I would argue rather that it is only in the absence of citizens' active participation in the process of progressively reinterpreting any constitutional right's meaning in changing situations that the courts can step in and make an (admittedly undemocratic) determination. Judicial determination could merely be a "court of last resort" for public input if indeed other avenues for participation were to be established. If that participation were established and itself constitutionally guaranteed, those constitutional *procedural* rights of participation in such areas, especially in environmental decision making, would have the opposite effect and the one Waldron seeks: empowering every generation to make their own decisions about how to apply environmental rights in their own situation.

In the United States at least, Waldron is correct that one reason for the overly dominant role of the courts in the protection and interpretation of human rights is the absence of other democratic mechanisms that citizens might employ to protect their rights. The U.S. Constitution describes one of only a few democratic systems not incorporating a process of national referendum for legislation, nor does it use a national recall process beyond impeachment, an entirely legislative function. Without even such relatively common avenues of citizen participation between elections, it is perhaps not surprising that U.S. citizens rely on courts too much and seem rather out of practice when it comes to democratic input into important constitutional questions such as reinterpreting, reinvigorating, or even reinventing rights. The absence of such participatory measures also might help to explain the overall low level of electoral participation in the United States when compared with that of other democratic nations. Given the absence of such constitutional measures to enhance citizen involvement, an approach arguably more conducive to fostering democratic participation would be to put *into* the U.S. Constitution a mechanism for referendum and recall, not, as Waldron suggests, to take the Bill of Rights *out* of the same document.[4]

Still, Waldron's concerns seem especially apt when it comes to considering environmental human rights and whether establishing them in constitutions might tie the hands of future citizens in making their own environmental choices. We have seen that when it comes to environmental use or abuse, future generations are uniquely vulnerable to the decisions of those who come before them, which is why establishing intergenerational environmental justice carries the urgency it does. The question then is whether establishing constitutional environmental human rights will have the chilling effect that Waldron suggests it will on the freedom of future generations to make their own collective decisions about how to do so.

As part of his affirmative answer, Waldron introduces into the discussion the idea of mistrust among citizens as a fundamental impetus behind the drive to put rights into constitutions. Earlier I quoted Nedelsky's passage that recognizes that to make rights constitutional is to accept both their consensual nature as a shared value as well as their risky status, both of which command the protection that inclusion in a constitution provides. As Waldron interprets it, however, the risk comes from our fellow citizens who might not agree with us about the "self-evident" nature of some rights claims and therefore might seek to undermine or otherwise challenge them. Waldron therefore argues that to put rights into constitutions is to introduce into political society an "attitude of mistrust of one's fellow citizens" that "does not sit particularly well with the aura of respect for their autonomy and responsibility" that is central both to the ideas of rights and democracy (Waldron, 1993, 27). Because constitutional provisions by their nature are meant to bind future generations to the values and practices incorporated within them, this mistrust is particularly directed at future citizens and their representatives. In terms of environmental rights, therefore, this lack of respect for future generations' abilities to make good environmental decisions seems clearly at odds with the whole idea of intergenerational environmental justice.

Waldron's argument is a provocative one against constitutional incorporation of substantive rights, and especially against constitutionally listed environmental human rights, because these seem far more intimately connected to the rights of future generations than any other actual or potential constitutional right, given the sustainability demands of environmental resources. I think that his arguments succeed only if constitutional environmental rights are construed in purely substantive terms. The rights to clean air, water, and soil

---

4 See Rourke, Hiskes, and Zirakzadeh (1992) for a discussion of national referendums referenda.

are obviously substantive in what they portend, although of course the questions of "how clean" or "what does clean mean" open them to some continuing interpretation. More important, as some recent constitutional provisions and documents such as Ksentini make clear, both scholars and constitutional framers have posited an intrinsic connection between substantive environmental human rights and procedural democratic rights to make environmental decisions.[5] It is through the constitutional incorporation of procedural human rights to manage their own environmental affairs that future generations are ensured democratic control and collective free choice over environmental decisions. In other words, by making the procedural environmental rights themselves part of the substantive constitutional right to a clean environment, virtually all of the negative effects on future decisions that Waldron envisions can be successfully anticipated and avoided.

Several recently written constitutions for states moving toward democracy have incorporated environmental human rights into them; some have included procedural environmental provisions – such as those suggested by Part III of the Ksentini Appendix – as well (Anton, 1998). It is not clear in every case what the motivation was for including procedural provisions, but I would contend that the connection between substantive and procedural environmental rights is itself an organic one, easily seen and adopted by authors of constitutional provisions and is so for particular reasons. Those reasons have to do with certain features of the natural environment that make democratically arrived at responses to it the most likely ones to be effective in guaranteeing a safe and productive relationship between humans and their natural habitat. In other words, democracy – as defined both by constitutionally prescribed substantive principles and guaranteed procedural rights – and environmentalism presume each other. I shall conclude with the exploration of this final relationship.

CONCLUSION: CONSTITUTIONAL ENVIRONMENTAL HUMAN RIGHTS AND INTERGENERATIONAL JUSTICE

As we have discussed them, constitutionally acknowledged procedural rights relating to the environment provide protection for *individual* citizens in the face of the *group* claims that substantive environmental rights make possible. This protection remains important because, as Nedelsky (2008) pointed out, all rights are relational in nature, and it is the duty of governments to protect

---

[5] For an examination of fifty constitutional provisions for substantive environmental rights see Donald K. Anton (1998), "Comparative Constitutional Language for Environmental Amendments to the Australian Constitution," www.elaw.org/resources/text.asp?ID=1082.

the equality of those relationships through the protection of individual rights. Substantive environmental rights grant to groups – both current and future – claims on living individual citizens that affect their behavior in terms on consumption, energy usage, and so forth. It is therefore crucial both in principle and in practice to protect individual rights to environmental goods as well. Procedural environmental rights are the mechanism with which to "balance" the power relationship individually between living citizens and their successor generations who exist as groups.

It is essential, therefore, that every living citizen have a voice in environmental decisions as a matter of right, because it is for the protection of the environmental *group* rights of the future that decisions will have to be made that limit the environmental choices of *each* living citizen today. Only through participatory democratic procedures can the equality between present and future generations be maintained, especially because the substantive guarantees provided by constitutional environmental rights already limit the choices of present citizens. Within that environment of constraint, however, the liberty of current citizens to participate in environmental decisions is the only way to ensure equal treatment of present and future generations. Future generations are guaranteed equal consideration by means of constitutionally mandated substantive environmental rights. Living citizens in return rely on the procedural right to participate in the engagement between democracy and nature as a way to ensure their equal treatment as well.

This balancing of procedural and substantive constitutional rights as the mechanism to protect present individual citizens and future generations indicates in a metaphorical way the general relationship between democracy and nature. As first understood by the natural law theorists of the seventeenth century, nature and its laws posited a role both for individual humans and the groups they established. For all the "state of nature" theorists beginning with Hobbes, people living without state or society could equally understand through reason what nature dictated, even if individually and in isolation they found that they were incapable of living in accordance with nature's laws. For Hobbes, and later Rousseau, this awareness both of nature's ways and our individual shortcomings presented essentially a tragic picture of man's future, either in terms of a loss of liberty or of peace. For Locke and the founding fathers of the United States, however, it is the laws of nature that make both peace and liberty possible, if politics is correctly employed to overcome the fundamental imbalance in power between every individual person and the sum of all others. That vision of politics is of course a democratic one, and the unique achievement of democracy is to bring together the essentially antagonistic values of interpersonal equality and individual liberty.

How well democracy has maintained its clever balance of equality and liberty is the storyline for another, never completely finished book, but what is provocative to recognize here is how similarly nature and democratic polities construe the relations between the individual persons and groups that populate each of them. Nature grants to each individual occupant the means with which to struggle for existence but reserves for species the evolutionary selection of individual adaptations that guarantee future group success. Similarly, democracy provides procedural guarantees of the equal right to liberty for individual persons to choose their own paths, but politics ultimately relies on collective choice to preserve the continuation of future generations of citizens and their institutions. Democratic politics makes collective choices with the guarantee of individual input and the right to play, but only the group determines – and is – the winner of the game.

So it is a "natural" thing to approach the issues of environmental protection, climate change, and sustainability within the conceptual frame of human rights, but only if those rights operate within a democratic framework. This is not necessarily to insist, as Michael Goodhart (2005) does, that human rights essentially reduce to democracy in all respects, nor must we either insist on (or necessarily reject) David Held's conception of an international, "cosmopolitan democracy" that establishes democratic procedures at all levels of global decision making (Held, 1995, 2004, 2006). The potential for global democratic practices such as Held describes ultimately depends on how far it is possible to expand our sense of community to embrace the entire world. For Held this means a new view of global, "cosmopolitan citizenship," an idea "not based on exclusive membership of a territorial community, but on the general rules and principles which can be entrenched and drawn upon in diverse settings" (Held and McGrew, 2007, 255). As a result of our exploration of moral cosmopolitanism in Chapter 4, I remain skeptical of human nature's ability to enlarge its communal sense that far, but in any case, democratic practices for environmental human rights need not wait for that adaptation to be accomplished.

Besides, not all human rights are necessarily democratic, nor do they all require democratic practices. Waldron (1993) and Goodin (1992), after all, are correct that many substantive human rights can be sustained without democratic institutions, but procedural environmental rights are what make the "natural" thing the "democratic" thing as well. No one recognized this any better than the framers of the U.S. Constitution, those products of both the idealism of the Enlightenment and the hard realism born of revolution and the failure of weak democracies. They sought "to secure the Blessings of Liberty to ourselves *and* to Posterity" (emphasis added). The Constitution that they ordained therefore included as its first amendments the rights necessary for *both* the procedural and substantive protection of liberty. In both aspects, it has succeeded for now more that 230 years in protecting individual citizens' rights as well as the rights of the future in many different areas of choice, decision, and action. It is now time to add one more such area: sustainable environmental choice, policy, and enforcement.

I have made many claims about democracy, constitutionalism, and environmental human rights in this chapter. Some of them likely remain controversial, but taken together they succeed in preparing a path for implementing environmental human rights and therefore for intergenerational environmental justice. To proceed down this path requires the exercise of substantial political will to make change in all nations, but those states with politics already defined by constitutions and democratic procedures are farther along that path than others. The same variable progress is evident in terms of how well individual countries at the present time have taken collective actions to ensure the environmental human rights of their future generations. Democratic nations are simply by definition more likely to be moving toward the constitutional measures necessary to secure environmental human rights and intergenerational environmental justice. It is particularly pressing, therefore, in this time of climate change that those democratic nations lead by example. That means both that their governments must adopt measures to protect the rights of future generations of citizens to clean air, water, and soil, and that their citizens must participate in the decisions and the sacrifices that their duty to the future requires. Nondemocratic nations must be urged to adopt democratic constitutions that ensure the same progress. Constitutionalism and democracy are not only the well-worn paths to "a more perfect Union," a "common defence," and "domestic tranquility" (the Preamble to the Constitution of the United States). They are the two most important requirements for global environmental health and justice as well.

7

Conclusion: Environmental Justice and the Emergent Future of Human Rights

We are caught in an inescapable network of mutuality, tied in a single garment of destiny.

Rev. Martin Luther King, Jr., *Letter from a Birmingham Jail*

Environmental justice across generations, it turns out, can be pursued only within the political context of constitutionalism and participatory democracy. Only in that political environment can substantive and procedural environmental human rights be protected and guaranteed for future as well as present generations of citizens, and it *is* citizens we speak of here, not simply all human beings. As we have seen, as opposed to altruism or even general moral duty, justice requires *political* identities – citizens of individual nations who recognize in each other and in the imagined faces of generations of their own future citizens a shared obligation to preserve their environment as part of a duty to maintain their own authenticity or group identity. All humans therefore possess environmental rights as (and only as) citizens of their own transgenerational national communities.

In her recent history of human rights, Lynn Hunt (2007, 27) disputes this conclusion, arguing that national identity alone cannot provide what she calls the necessary "disposition toward other people" and "set of convictions about what people are like" that together form the basis of both human rights and justice. For her, that disposition and set of convictions are what make human empathy possible, and as the foundation of human rights, empathy is both necessary and more intimate than shared national identity. She therefore concludes, "what might be termed 'imagined empathy' serves as the foundation of human rights rather than nationalism" (p. 32).

Even if this point were granted, however, Chapter 4 has argued that it is difficult to see how empathy can be extended toward future generations unless it is alloyed with a national community attachment. Without this sense of shared identity with future persons, justice across generations cannot be based on human rights. Making that identification political by locating it within the political body of the nation state – still the addressee of human rights – is what makes environmental justice amenable to the strictures of human rights. Human rights might indeed require only empathy, but environmental justice that is based on human rights requires the sharing of political identity across time that national constitutions, political institutions, and democratic practices provide.

Still, the overall thrust of Hunt's foundation of human rights is important for my argument as well. The title of her book, *Inventing Human Rights*, is daring for its implication that the process of invention is not only historical but ongoing. Although Hunt's book is a history, it carries an admonition that the concept and practices of human rights are organic and evolving in our day as well. As she claims in her first chapter, human rights are born of the human interactions of empathetic and autonomous individual persons creating a new social context (p. 34). From those interactions emerge all social changes, including the acceptance of human rights as authoritative in political affairs. In short, all human rights are emergent phenomena, including those not yet invented. As human relationships evolve, so too will our understanding of which human rights exist and how they are to be expressed, defended, and secured.

Environmental human rights, as I have explicated them in this book, clearly constitute a newly emergent human right, one especially tied to the concept and practice of social justice, specifically environmental justice aimed at future generations. This is a new understanding of both human rights and of environmental justice, one that relies heavily on the acceptance of several other new or otherwise controversial conceptualizations that I have explored in previous chapters. That reliance, I recognize, makes this understanding of human rights and environmental justice itself controversial. The concepts of a relationally defined self-identity, emergent harms or risks, and reflexive reciprocity, to name but a few, are not the terms usually found in a characterization of the foundation of human rights or in a defense of a new right.

Ultimately then, my argument for environmental human rights and for intergenerational environmental justice relies on the acceptability of emergent human rights as a concept on which to build. As I introduced them in Chapter 2, the concept of emergent human rights opens the door to two specific innovations or theoretical directions within human rights theory. First, the concept of emergent rights provides a new foundation for human rights that further distinguishes them from other ideas of rights, whether called "natural" or "inalienable." Second, emergent rights supply an impetus toward accepting the idea of group rights, because if rights are emergent in character they imply the existence of individual interactions within groups as necessary for the emergence of rights. I shall close my exploration with a brief discussion of the implications of both of these innovations for the future of human rights.

THE EMERGENT FOUNDATION OF HUMAN RIGHTS

As I presented the case for environmental human rights in Chapter 2, I argued that their emergent character is suggested by three aspects, the first of which applies equally to all human rights, the latter two are specifically (although not exclusively) relevant to environmental rights. The first has to do with human identity as the source of rights, the latter two with the types of risks that give rise first to environmental rights and second to their correlative duties.

Drawing from several different strains of contemporary thought, including feminism, communitarianism, Marxism, and postmodernism, individual human identity today is widely viewed as both malleable and the result of relationships and interactions between persons and their environments. Those environments include other people, social structures, political institutions, and, I argued, a natural order seen as far more ecologically interconnected than previously thought during the seed time of rights theory in the seventeenth century. Our understanding of human identity as relational and contextual means that when those relationships and contexts change, fundamental identity changes are also likely. For example, as the political institutions of democracy have grown and been disseminated across the globe during the past three centuries, tangible changes in how individual people view themselves and their relationships to others have also occurred.

Similarly, whereas rights theorists in the seventeenth century projected that the first step toward political liberty was away from nature – to leave the "state of nature" – human rights theorists today understand that although rights are rooted in society, they are also affected by our natural needs and our interactions with nature. The science of ecology has taught us that our interconnection with nature means we can never leave it or assume that it is somehow separated from our private lives. Our impact on nature is immediate and emanates from our every private decision about how to eat, travel, heat our homes, adorn our bodies, and so forth. Those impacts are felt by others as well and with the same immediacy.

The impact of our private choices on nature and on others underlies the second and third aspects of emergent rights. Living in modern society connects us with others in ways intensified by every innovation in technology, communication, the public understanding of health, and even politics. To live in modernity is to feel the risks that our environment impinges, and especially how the choices of others impact our own security or sense of being at risk. In other words, as we saw in Chapter 2, risks emerge at the collective level and present a new kind of emergent harm, for which we need rights to protect us. The duties that are correlated with those rights differ as well, both because they are associated with new emergent risks and because they presume a different, collective sense of obligation that cannot be reduced entirely to individual persons or duties.

With this understanding of how three essential and foundational aspects of rights are themselves both new and emergent, it should not surprise us that many rights today seem new themselves. If rights are the product of human relationships, risks, and obligations, and those three sources manifest changed natures, our rights change with them. New rights, in other words, emerge from changed foundations. Where once we understood the human reason of private individual persons to be the source of rights, now we realize with Hunt that both feelings and the shared experiences of individuals-in-relations (to again borrow Carol Gould's term) are what make human rights self-evident. As Hunt says (p. 34), "[F]or human rights to become self-evident, ordinary people had to have new understandings that came from new kinds of feelings."

Human rights are the products then of human identity, but that identity itself is forged in relationships with others, with institutions and institutionalized power, and with nature – relationships that are themselves always changing. It would be illogical to assume then that amidst all this flux and growth, human rights would remain static. Human rights change, and new rights appear not because they are simply socially constructed, or because, as Ignatieff (2001, 83) pragmatically argues, because history has proved we need them. Rather, human rights grow and evolve as the human relationships from which they emerge change the ways in which we relate to each other, our politics, and our natural world. The relationships make us who we are, and in so doing define the rights we not only need but also deserve as beings capable of those relationships.

The most recent of those relationships to emerge is with our natural environment, or perhaps it is better to say that this relationship has been most recently and consciously in flux. Global warming and climate change have made it abundantly clear that the human impact on the environment is an emergent one, the product of uncounted individual decisions and choices on one hand, and public policies and political omissions on the other, which make every one of us responsible for putting all the rest of us in a new situation of risk, and not only "all of us," but those who come after us as well. Both ourselves and those who succeed us have rights and obligations defined by this new relationship to nature.

These rights and obligations have increased as democracy has spread. Kristin Shrader-Frechette argues that particularly citizens in democratic societies cannot escape what she calls "the responsibility argument" when it comes to saving the environment or improving public health. Democracies through the guarantees of constitutionalism offer citizens the opportunity to check the power of governments and all institutions that either countenance or perpetuate new environmental harms. As citizens empowered to effect governmental and organizational decision making for the environment and for public health, they must recognize that when "some institution enjoys unchecked power, democratic peoples ultimately should also blame themselves, and not merely scapegoat the institution" (2007, 11).

Our new relationship with nature has made environmental rights possible at the same time that our democratic constitutions have made our environmental obligations impossible to shirk. For democratic citizens charged with the constitutional duty to check the power of government, this means we have the right – and the obligation – to demand public action aimed at providing clean air, water, and soil. The harms that await us in terms of public health as the consequences of inaction are what prove the existence of our environmental rights. Rights are necessarily the legal response to harms, real or potential. The fact that they are new and collective harms that do not fit within the traditional individualist language of either rights or responsibility do not, as we saw in Chapter 2, alter the equation of rights as a response to harm. New harms demand new rights. Because they are emergent harms, the rights that they begat will share their emergent ontological nature.

The right to claim environmental action from democratic governments also carries the new obligation both publicly to do so and also to respect the similar rights of others. These rights, as we have seen in the last chapter, are both substantive and procedural. Their substance is defined by the environmental harms against which they are aimed; their procedural content is defined by democratic constitutions and also, as we have seen, by the parallelism between democracy and nature in the essentially emergent, collective processes such as public will or evolution that respectively define them.

Protecting environmental rights also requires sacrifice on the part of all of society, as is customarily the case with rights, but with a significant difference. Environmental rights posit a relationship (defined by rights and duties) with a usually ignored set of others – future generations. Furthermore, environmental rights not only insist that future persons will actually have the same rights as us but also, much more significantly, that we have obligations toward them already because of those rights, even though their bearers do not yet exist. This reciprocity between present and future generations in terms of their environmental rights is what makes intergenerational environmental justice possible, and it is a reciprocity consisting fully of rights, not just duties. As we saw in Chapter 3, by protecting the rights of the future, we also significantly protect our own, and it is this "reflexive reciprocity" that makes environmental justice self-interested and not merely altruistic. As such, environmental justice satisfies the old Platonic requirement (and hope) that justice is both good and in our interest. It is therefore, as Socrates insisted, the "noblest" virtue as well: it deserves "to be loved both for its own sake, and for what comes of it, if you mean to be perfectly happy" (Republic, Bk II, para. 10).

Of course, the reciprocity that renders transgenerational justice based on environmental human rights not only virtuous but also self-interested (and therefore noble) is somewhat abstract. It requires us to recognize in a real way the participation in a reciprocal relationship with us by others whose existence remains only theoretical. Future persons must join and be recognized by us as actual, tangible members of our reciprocal "network of mutuality," as Martin Luther King refers to it in the quotation that begins this chapter. Until that recognition becomes pervasive, environmental justice is not possible, just as King recognized that racial justice waits on the concrete realization that all races share the same relationship. We saw that nothing furthers the recognition of our interconnection (or mutuality) more than current environmental issues, but to extend that sense of connection to the future requires that we recognize the rights of those who come after us. Logically, those rights must be group rights – in this case of a very abstract group – and so the recognition on which environmental justice awaits is made even more difficult.

ENVIRONMENTAL JUSTICE AS A RIGHT OF THE HUMAN GROUP

Treating human identity as a matter of relationships naturally stimulates a focus on the groups to which individuals belong. To claim as I have, however, that new human rights emerge from these groups promotes a very novel interpretation of so-called group rights. For the past 50 years or so, especially in Western societies that profess an individualist ontology of human rights, group rights have come to refer to rights claimed by indigenous groups within individualist societies who view themselves (or are viewed) as somehow "different." Members of such a group claim a shared and common identity that diverges in ways important enough to warrant protecting it from the influences or pressures from the rest of society. My argument for environmental human rights has presented an opposite ontology for how group environmental rights should be viewed – not as belonging to people "different" from us, but to those who are entitled to them owing to their similarity and kinship to present generations.

Group human rights remain controversial largely because of their association with identity in what has become known as "identity politics." Such politics is filled with contentiousness precisely because of an inequality of power between the group sharing an identity and an external, often national, group, usually one that is heterogeneous enough so that its members often (perhaps mistakenly) define their identities primarily in individualist terms. In other words, minorities (i.e., those suffering from the inequality of power) become defined – or define themselves – as minority *groups*. The irony, of course, is that in individualist societies like the United States, minority politics is often the struggle to achieve either home rule or other benefits to enable group members one day to leave the group and be recognized solely as individual persons within the larger society. Group rights are claimed then in response to an inequality of power that for a variety of reasons leads a group to establish a group identity either as a protective device or as a tool by which to promote its own members. The two keys here are inequality and difference.

Whatever one might think of the claims of group human rights or of identity politics in general, it is important to recognize how the group identity of future generations differs from group identity within the struggle known as identity politics. True, future generations stand in a relation of inequality to present ones; indeed, the vulnerability of those not yet living to those who are alive is prodigious. The environmental decisions that we make today will have vast impact on the future; our power superiority over future generations is virtually complete. Future generations are always a minority group compared with the living, who have the power to affect them. What can equalize power between generations, between the groups that live today and the groups that will succeed them? What can grant them equal human rights to a safe environment? Not a recognition of how we or they differ from each other, but only an acknowledgment of how we are alike. For environmental human rights to be shared equally by all generations, we must recognize how we are the same.

As I argued in Chapter 4, this recognition of the sameness that underwrites respect for human rights is limited within the bounds of the human capacity for empathy, as Hunt (2007) also recognizes. It is simply not possible for humans to care equally about each other person, much less each other *future* person; our empathetic successes are bounded by the limits of kinship, friendship, and citizenship. We are able to care about our *own* future generations, and not just our children and heirs but also about those who share our political identity and our political institutions – our future fellow citizens. We can acknowledge their group human rights to a safe environment, and doing so, I have argued, is at least a very important start in reaching a global consensus on environmental human rights, and indeed on human rights in general.

This sense of our group obligations to protect the group rights of our successor generations is a powerful foundation for an environmental justice that extends into the future. Its power compels us to view ourselves and our rights always within the context of the group to which we – and our successors – belong. Even though we acknowledge their rights because of our shared similarities and shared membership, it is unquestionable that this acknowledgment validates the concept of group rights in general, and in a completely new way that also encompasses the group rights of groups characterized by their difference from us. The environmental rights of our national community are shared by those living and future members of *all* national communities, as different or alien as they might seem in our eyes. We possess environmental human rights as members of our national community, which differs in important ways – physical, cultural, and political – from other national communities, but citizens of those communities possess environmental rights and obligations vis-à-vis their future generations as well.

There is no denying that environmental human rights valorize the concept of group rights as well as that of emergent human rights. This is the conceptual innovation that environmental human rights bring to the global discourse of rights; it is, if you will, what "emerges" from our acceptance of environmental rights.

Two reasons emerge that make it evident why this group focus is entirely appropriate when considering the relationships of humans to their natural environment. First, of course, and as discussed in Chapter 1, like any focus on the environment, environmental rights require that we think of long-term effects engaging future generations. Doing so leads ineluctably to the conclusion that because they do not yet exist we cannot think of future persons as real persons, but only as constituting a somewhat abstract group.

Second, within nature important processes that define the ecosystem and our place within it operate at both individual and group levels. Whether we focus on large-scale phenomena such as evolution or climatic change, or more localized effects such as one's species' place in the food chain or the need to "thin the herd," both groups and individual persons represent relevant levels of analysis. Philosophers of science disagree about whether within evolutionary processes it is the gene, the individual living creature, or the species that is the mechanism of natural selection, just as climatologists and others argue over whether the human species as a whole or only those cultures adopting "modern" modes of consumption are responsible for climate change. The arguments themselves indicate the presence of evidence supporting a dual focus on both individual and group levels.

The point is that when confronting nature, one cannot ignore the impact either of individual or group effects; therefore it should come as no surprise that when we explore the rights that emerge from our encounter with nature, it is clear that some of those rights we possess only as members of groups. These are the rights I have termed "environmental human rights." Their emergence in both our consciousness and our politics surely ushers in a new chapter in the development of human rights as a central focus of human political endeavor.

Because incorporating environmental rights into our decision process is so manifestly a political endeavor, it is thereby clear that we are operating within the domain of justice, the goal or purpose of all political organization. Environmental justice is an increasingly important and necessary part of our political purpose, for without it no adequate response to global warming and climate change is conceivable. Achieving justice is a human ideal as old as the species itself, and one on which the conscious theorizing about politics began with the ancient Greeks. Today, environmental justice requires that we also must engage the futures of both our nations and our species in a way that is more conscious of the rightful claims the future makes on the occupiers of the present. Intergenerational environmental justice must become a central political goal of all nations. To serve them in their pursuit, I offer the concept and muscular political language of environmental human rights. Like all human rights, environmental rights are born of human relationships with others individually and in groups, but because they also incorporate the rights of future groups, environmental human rights are shared by individual people first as citizens and also, finally, as members of a single entity, the human group.

References

Anton, Donald K. (1998). "Comparative Constitutional Language for Environmental Amendments to the Australian Constitution." www.elaw.org/resources/text.asp? ID=1082.

Arat, Zehra F. Kabalskal (2006). "Forging a Global Culture of Human Rights: Origins and Prospects of the International Bill of Rights." *Human Rights Quarterly* 28: 416–437.

Arendt, Hannah ([1951], 1979). *The Origins of Totalitarianism*. New York: Harcourt, Brace, and Jovanovich.

Arendt, Hannah (1965). *Eichmann in Jerusalem: A Report on the Banality of Evil*. New York: Penguin Books.

Attfield, Robin (1999). *The Ethics of the Global Environment*. West Lafayette, IN: Purdue University Press.

Baier, Annette (1981). "The Rights of Past and Future Persons," in Ernest Partridge, ed., *Responsibilities to Future Generations*. Buffalo: Prometheus; 171–183.

Ball, Terence (1985). "The Incoherence of Intergenerational Justice." *Inquiry* 28: 321–337.

Barry, Brian (1989). *Theories of Justice*. Berkeley: University of California Press.

Barry, Brian (1995). *Justice as Impartiality*. New York: Oxford University Press.

Barry, Brian (1999). "Sustainability and Intergenerational Justice," in Andrew Dobson, ed., *Fairness and Futurity*. New York: Oxford University Press.

Baxi, Upenda (2002). *The Future of Human Rights*. Oxford: Oxford University Press.

Beck, Ulrick (1992). *Risk Society*. London: Sage Publications.

Becker, Lawrence C. (1986). *Reciprocity*. New York: Routledge and Kegan Paul.

Beckerman, Wilfred (1997). "Debate: Intergenerational Equity and the Environment." *Journal of Political Philosophy* 5: 392–405.

Beckerman, Wilfred (1999). "Sustainable Development and Our Obligations to Future Generations," in Andrew Dobson, ed., *Fairness and Futurity*. New York: Oxford University Press.

Beckerman, Wilfred and Joanna Pasek (2001). *Justice, Posterity, and the Environment*. Oxford: Oxford University Press.

Bell, Derek (2004). "Environmental Justice and Rawls' Difference Principle." *Environmental Ethics* 26: 287–306.

Benhabib, Seyla (2002). *The Claims of Culture*. Princeton, NJ: Princeton University Press.

Benjamin, Jessica (1988). *The Bonds of Love: Psychoanalysis, Feminism, and the Problem of Domination*. New York: Pantheon.

Berlin, Isaiah (1969). *Four Essays on Liberty*. Oxford: Oxford University Press.

Boyle, Alan (1996). "The Role of International Human Rights Law in the Protection of the Environment," in Alan Boyle and Michael Anderson, eds., *Human Rights Approaches to Environmental Protection*. Oxford: Clarendon Press; 43–70.

Brysk, Alyson (2002). *Globalization and Human Rights*. Berkeley: University of California Press.

Buchanan, Allen (1990). "Justice as Reciprocity versus Subject-centered Justice." *Philosophy & Public Affairs* 19: 227–252.

Burke, Edmund (1910). *Reflections on the Revolution in France*. London: Macmillan.

Chun, Lin (2001). "Human Rights and Democracy: The Case for Decoupling." *International Journal of Human Rights* 5: 19–44.

Collins-Chobanian, Shari (2000). "Beyond Sax and Welfare Interests." *Environmental Ethics* 22: 133–148.

Connolly, William E. (1991). *Identity/Difference: Democratic Negotiations of Political Paradox*. Ithaca: Cornell University Press.

Cranston, Maurice (1967). "Human Rights, Real and Supposed," in D. D. Raphael, ed., *Political Theory and the Rights of Man*. Bloomington, IN: Indiana University Press.

Crawford, James (1988). *The Rights of Peoples*. Oxford: Clarendon Press.

Dagger, Richard (1985). "Rights, Boundaries, and the Bonds of Community: A Qualified Defense of Moral Parochialism." *American Political Science Review* 79: 436–448.

De-Shalit, Avner (1995). *Why Posterity Matters*. New York: Routledge.

Dobson, Andrew (1996). "Democratising Green Theory: Preconditions and Principles," in Brian Doherty and Marius deGeus, eds., *Democracy and Green Political Thought*. London: Routledge.

Dodds, Graham G. (2005). "Political Apologies: Chronological List." www.upenn.edu/pnc/politicalapologies.html.

Donnelly, Jack (1989). *Universal Human Rights in Theory and Practice*. Ithaca: Cornell University Press.

Donnelly, Jack (2007). "The Relative Universality of Human Rights." *Human Rights Quarterly* 29: 281–306.

Dowding, Keith and Martin van Hees (2003). "The Construction of Rights," *American Political Science Review* 97: 281–294.

Dryzek, John (1997). *The Politics of the Earth*. Oxford, England: Oxford University Press.

Dworkin, Ronald (1977). *Taking Rights Seriously*. Cambridge, MA: Harvard University Press.

Eagleton, Terry (1999). "Local and Global," in Obrad Savic, ed., *The Politics of Human Rights*. London: Verso; 245–257.

Elshtain, Jean Bethke (1995). *Democracy on Trial*. New York: Basic Books.

Ezra, Ovadia (2008). "Human Rights: The Immanent Dichotomy." *Journal of Human Rights* 7: 207–223.

Falk, Richard (2002). "Interpreting the Interaction of Global Markets and Human Rights," in Alyson Brysk, ed., *Globalization and Human Rights*. Berkeley: University of California Press; 61–76.

Feinberg, Joel (1970). *Doing and Deserving*. Princeton, NJ: Princeton University Press.

Feinberg, Joel (1980a). "The Rights of Animals and Unborn Generations," in Joel Feinberg, *Rights, Justice, and the Bounds of Liberty*. Princeton, NJ: Princeton; 159–184.

Feinberg, Joel (1980b). *Rights, Justice, and the Bounds of Liberty*. Princeton, NJ: Princeton University Press.

Francis, Lesley Pickering (2003). "Global Systemic Problems and Interconnected Duties." *Environmental Ethics* 25: 115–208.

French, Peter (1984). *Collective and Corporate Responsibility*. New York: Columbia University Press.

Garcia, Frank (1999). "The Global Market and Human Rights: Trading Away the Human Rights Principle." *Brooklyn Journal of International Law* 25, 51 www.westlaw.com.

Gauthier, David (1986). *Morals by Agreement*. Oxford: Oxford University Press.

Gewirth, Alan (1978). *Reason and Morality*. Chicago: University of Chicago Press.

Gewirth, Alan (1996). *The Community of Rights*. Chicago: University of Chicago Press.

Gibbard, Allan (1991). "Constructing Justice." *Philosophy & Public Affairs* 20: 264–279.

Gilligan, Carol (1982). *In a Different Voice: Psychological Theory and Women's Development*. Cambridge, MA: Harvard University Press.

Glendon, Mary Ann (1993). *Rights Talk*. New York: Free Press.

Golding, Martin P. (1981). "Obligations to Future Generations," in Ernest Partridge, ed., *Responsibilities to Future Generations*. Buffalo: Prometheus 61–72.

Goodhart, Michael (2003). "Origins and Universality in the Human Rights Debates: Cultural Essentialism and the Challenge of Globalization." *Human Rights Quarterly* 25: 935–964.

Goodhart, Michael (2005). *Democracy as Human Rights: Freedom and Equality in the Age of Globalization*. New York: Routledge.

Goodin, Robert (1992). *Green Political Theory*. Cambridge: Polity Press.

Goodin, Robert E. (1985). *Protecting the Vulnerable*. Chicago: University of Chicago Press.

Gore, Al (2006). *An Inconvenient Truth*. New York: Rodale Press.

Gould, Carol C. (1988). *Rethinking Democracy*. New York: Cambridge University Press.

Gould, Carol C. (2004). *Globalizing Democracy and Human Rights*. New York: Cambridge University Press.

Gutmann, Amy and Dennis Thompson (1996). *Democracy and Disagreement*. Cambridge, MA: Harvard University Press.

Handl, Gunther (1992). "Human Rights and the Protection of the Environment: A Mildly Revisionist View," in Antonio Augusto Cancado Trindade, ed., *Human Rights, Sustainable Development and the Environment*. San Jose, Costa Rica: Instituto Interamericano de Derechos Humanos.

Hannum, Hurst (1998). "The Right of Self-Determination in the Twenty-first Century." *Washington and Lee Law Review*. Summer: 773–780.

Harman, Gilbert (1980). "Moral Relativism as a Foundation for Natural Rights." *Journal of Libertarian Studies* 4: 367–371.

Hart, H. L. A. (1955). "Are There Any Natural Rights?" *Philosophical Review*, 64: 175–191.

Hayward, Tim (2005). *Constitutional Environmental Rights*. Oxford: Oxford University Press.

Held, David (1995). *Democracy and the Global Order: From the Modern State to Cosmopolitan Governance*. Cambridge: Polity Press.

Held, David (2004). *Global Covenant*. Cambridge, England: Polity Press.

Held, David (2006). *Models of Democracy*, 3rd edition. Cambridge: Polity Press.

Held, David and Anthony McGrew, eds. (2007). *Globalization Theory: Approaches and Controversies*. Cambridge: Polity Press.

Herz, Richard (2000). "Litigating Environmental Abuses under the Alien Tort Claims Act: A Practical Assessment." *Virginia Journal of International Law* 40 (Winter) 545–632.

Hiskes, Richard P. (1998). *Democracy, Risk and Community: Technological Hazards and the Evolution of Liberalism*. New York: Oxford University Press.

Holder, Cindy (2006). "Self-Determination as a Universal Human Right." *Human Rights Review* 7: 5–18.

Holmes, Stephen and Cass Sunstein (1999). *The Cost of Rights*. New York: W. W. Norton.

Howard-Hassman, Rhoda (2004). "Culture, Human Rights, and the Politics of Resentment in the Era of Globalization." *Human Rights Review* 6: 5–26.

Howard-Hassmann, Rhoda (2005). "The Second Great Transformation: Human Rights Leapfrogging in the Era of Globalization." *Human Rights Quarterly* 27: 1–40.

Hume, David (1896). *A Treatise of Human Nature*, L. A. Selby-Bigge, ed. Oxford: Clarendon Press.

Hunt, Lynn (2007). *Inventing Human Rights: A History*. New York: W. W. Norton.

Ignatieff, Michael (2001). *Human Rights as Politics and Idolatry*. Princeton, NJ: Princeton University Press.

Ignatieff, Michael (1984). *The Needs of Strangers*. New York: Basic Books.

Ignatieff, Michael (1999). "Human Rights: The Midlife Crisis" [Review Essay]. *New York Review of Books* 46: 9(20 May)58–62.

Ikenberry, G. John (2007). "Globalization as American Hegemony," in David Held and Anthony McGrew, eds., *Globalization Theory: Approaches and Controversies*. Cambridge, England: Polity Press, 41–61.

Ishay, Micheline (2004). *The History of Human Rights*. Berkeley: University of California Press.

Kant, Immanuel (1959). *Foundation of the Metaphysics of Morals*. Translated by Lewis White Beck. Indianapolis: Bobbs-Merrill.

Keck, Margaret E. and Kathryn Sikkink (1998). *Activists beyond Borders*. Ithaca, NY: Cornell University Press.

Keller, Evelyn Fox (1989). "The Gender/Science System: Or, Is Sex to Gender as Nature Is to Science?" *Hypatia* 2 (3): 37–49.

Keohane, Robert O. and Joseph S. Nye Jr. (2000). "Globalization: What's New? What's Not? (and So What?)." *Foreign Policy* 118 (Spring): 104–119.

Klabbers, Jan (2006). "The Right to be Taken Seriously: Self-Determination in International Law." *Human Rights Quarterly* 28: 186–206.

Korten, David C. (1995). *When Corporations Rule the World.* West Hartford, CT: Kumarian Press.

Kristeva, Julia (1981). "Women Can Never be Defined," in Elaine Marks and Isabelle de Courtivron, eds., *New French Feminisms.* New York: Schocken Books.

Ksentini, Fatma (1994). *Final Report of the UN Sub-Commission on Human Rights and the Environment.* UNDoc.E/CN.4Sub.2/1994/9.

Kymlicka, Will (1989). *Liberalism, Community and Culture.* Oxford: Clarendon Press.

Kymlicka, Will (1995a). *Multicultural Citizenship.* New York: Oxford University Press.

Kymlicka, Will (1995b). *The Rights of Minority Cultures.* New York: Oxford University Press.

Kymlicka, Will (1996). "The Good, the Bad, and the Intolerable: Minority Group Rights." *Dissent.* Summer 43: 22–30.

Lazarus, Richard J. (2004). *The Making of Environmental Law.* Chicago: University of Chicago Press.

MacIntyre, Alasdair (1984). *Is Patriotism a Virtue?* Lawrence, KA: University Press of Kansas.

Marrus, Michael R. (2007). "Official Apologies and the Quest for Historical Justice." *Journal of Human Rights* 6: 75–105.

Martin, Rex and David A. Reidy, eds. (2006). *Rawls's Law of Peoples.* New York: Oxford University Press.

Mason, Andrew (1997). "Special Obligations to Compatriots." *Ethics* 107: 427–447.

May, Larry (1987). *The Morality of Groups.* South Bend, IN: University of Notre Dame Press.

May, Larry (1992). *Sharing Responsibility.* Chicago: University of Chicago Press.

Meehan, M. Johanna (2001). "Into the Sunlight: A Pragmatic Account of the Self," in William Rehg and James Bowman, eds., *Pluralism and the Pragmatic Turn.* Cambridge, MA: MIT Press.

Meyers, Diana T. (1985). *Inalienable Rights: A Defense.* New York: Columbia University Press.

Mill, J. S. (1978 [1869]). *On Liberty,* Elizabeth Rappaport, ed. Indianapolis: Hackett Publishing.

Miller, David (1988). "The Ethical Significance of Nationality." *Ethics* 98: 647–662.

Miller, David (1995). *On Nationality.* Oxford: Oxford University Press.

Miller, David (1997). "Nationality: Some Replies." *Journal of Applied Philosophy* 14: 69–82.

Miller, David (1999). "Social Justice and Environmental Goods," in Andrew Dobson, ed., *Fairness and Futurity.* New York: Oxford University Press.

Minow, Martha (1998). *Between Vengeance and Forgiveness.* Boston: Beacon Press.

Monshipouri, Mahmood, et. al. (2003). *Constructing Human Rights in the Age of Globalization.* Armonk, NY: M. E. Sharpe Books.

Moore, Margaret (2001). *The Ethics of Nationalism.* Oxford: Oxford University Press.

Nedelsky, Jennifer (2008). "Reconceiving Rights and Constitutionalism." *Journal of Human Rights* 7: 139–173.

Nickel, James W. (1993). "The Human Right to a Safe Environment: Philosophical Perspectives on its Scope and Justification." *Yale Journal of International Law* 18: 281–285.

Nickel, James W. (2002). "Is Today's International Human Rights System a Global Governance Regime?" *Journal of Ethics* 6: 353–371.

Nwogu, Nneoma (2007). "Regional Integration as an Instrument of Human Rights: Reconceptualizing ECOWAS." *Journal of Human Rights* 6: 345–360.

O'Neill, John (1994). "Should Communitarians be Nationalists?" *Journal of Applied Philosophy* 11: 135–143.

Pagden, Anthony (2003). Human Rights, Natural Rights, and Europe's Imperial Legacy." *Political Theory* 31: 171–199.

Parfit, Derek (1984). *Reasons and Persons*. Oxford: Oxford University Press.

Parker, Karen (2000). "Understanding Self-Determination: The Basics." Presented at the First International Conference on the Right to Self-Determination, United Nations, Geneva, August.

Pitkin, Hannah Fenichel (1998). *The Attack of the Blob: Hannah Arendt's Concept of the Political*. Chicago: University of Chicago Press.

Rawls, John (1971). *A Theory of Justice*. Cambridge, MA: Harvard University Press.

Rawls, John (1999). *The Law of Peoples*. Cambridge, MA: Harvard University Press.

Risse, Thomas, Stephen C. Ropp, and Kathryn Sikkink (1999). *The Power of Human Rights: International Norms and Domestic Change*. Cambridge: Cambridge University Press.

Robertson, Roland and David Inglis (1992). *Globalization: Social Theory and Global Culture (Theorizing Society)*. New York: Open University Press.

Robinson, Mary (2003). "Globalization and Human Rights." Address at the 21st Century Trust Seminar on Globalization: Rhetoric, Reality, and International Politics. U.S. Congress, Washington DC, 31 October, 2003.

Rorty, Richard (1993). "Human Rights, Rationality, and Sentimentality, in Stephen Shute and Susan Hurley, eds., *On Human Rights: Oxford Amnesty Lectures 1993*. New York: Basic Books.

Rosenau, James N. (2002). "The Drama of Human Rights in a Turbulent, Globalized World," in Alyson Brysk, ed., *Globalization and Human Rights*. Berkeley: University of California Press; 148–167.

Rosenblum, Nancy, ed. (1982). *Liberalism and the Moral Life*. Cambridge, MA: Harvard University Press.

Rourke, John, Richard P. Hiskes, Cyrus Ernesto Zirakzadeh (1992). *Direct Democracy and International Politics*. Boulder, CO: Lynne Rienner Publishers.

Ruddick, Sara (1989). *Maternal Thinking: Towards a Politics of Peace*. Boston: Beacon Press.

Sandel, Michael J. (1982). *Liberalism and the Limits of Justice*. Cambridge: Cambridge University Press.

Savic, Obrad (1999). *The Politics of Human Rights*. London: Verso Books.

Sax, Joseph L. (1990). "The Search for Environmental Rights." *Journal of Land Use and Environmental Law* 6: 90–103.

Schumaker, Millard (1992). *Sharing without Reckoning: Imperfect Right and the Norms of Reciprocity*. Canada: Wilfrid Laurier University Press.

Shrader-Frechette, Kristin (2002). *Environmental Justice*. New York: Oxford University Press.

Shrader-Frechette, Kristin (2007). *Taking Action, Saving Lives: Our Duties to Protect Environmental and Public Health*. New York: Oxford University Press.

Shue, Henry (1980). *Basic Rights*. Princeton, NJ: Princeton University Press.

Simmons, A. John (1996). "Associative Political Obligations." *Ethics* 106: 247–273.

Singer, Peter (1975). *Animal Liberation*. New York: Random House.

Smiley, Marion (1992). *Moral Responsibility and the Boundaries of Community*. Chicago: University of Chicago Press.

Steiner, Henry J. and Philip Alston (2000). *International Human Rights in Context*, 2nd edition. Oxford, England: Oxford University Press.

Tamir, Yael (1993). *Liberal Nationalism*. Princeton, NJ: Princeton University Press.

Taylor, Charles (1989). *Sources of the Self*. Cambridge, MA: Harvard University Press.

Taylor, Charles (1992). "'Multiculturalism' and the Politics of Recognition," in Amy Gutmann, ed., *Multiculturalism*. Princeton, NJ: Princeton University Press.

Thompson, Dennis F. (1980). "Moral Responsibility of Public Officials: The Problem of Many Hands." *American Political Science Review* 74: 905–916.

Thompson, Janna (2002). *Taking Responsibility for the Past: Reparation and Historical Injustice*. Cambridge: Polity Press.

Thomson, Judith J. (1990). *The Realm of Rights*. Cambridge, MA: Harvard University Press.

UNECE (2007). Kiev Protocol. www.UNECE.org/env/pp/prtr.htm.

Waldron, Jeremy (1987). *Nonsense Upon Stilts: Bentham, Burke and Marx on the Rights of Man*. London: Methuen.

Waldron, Jeremy (1993). "A Rights-based Critique of Constitutional Rights." *Oxford Journal of Legal Studies* 13: 18–51.

Weinstock, Daniel M. (1996). "Is There a Moral Case for Nationalism?" *Journal of Applied Philosophy* 13: 87–100.

Weiss, Edith Brown (1989). *In Fairness to Future Generations: International Law, Common Patrimony, and Intergenerational Equity*. Irvington-on-Hudson, NY: Transnational Publishers.

Wellman, Carl (1995). *Real Rights*. New York: Oxford University Press.

Winston, Morton E., ed. (1989). *The Philosophy of Human Rights*. Belmont, CA: Wadsworth Publishing.

Wolin, Sheldon (1960, 2004). *Politics and Vision: Continuity and Innovation in Western Political Thought* (1st and 2nd editions). Princeton, NJ: Princeton University Press.

World Commission on Environment and Development (1987). *Our Common Future* (Brundtland Report). New York: Oxford University Press.

Young, Iris (1990). *Justice and the Politics of Difference*. Princeton, NJ: Princeton University Press.

Young, Iris (2000). *Inclusion and Democracy*. Oxford: Oxford University Press.

Young, Iris (2002). "Two Concepts of Self-Determination," in Austin Sarat and Thomas R. Kearns, eds., *Human Rights: Concepts, Contests, Contingencies*. Ann Arbor, MI: University of Michigan Press.

Index